IROQUOIS CRAFTS

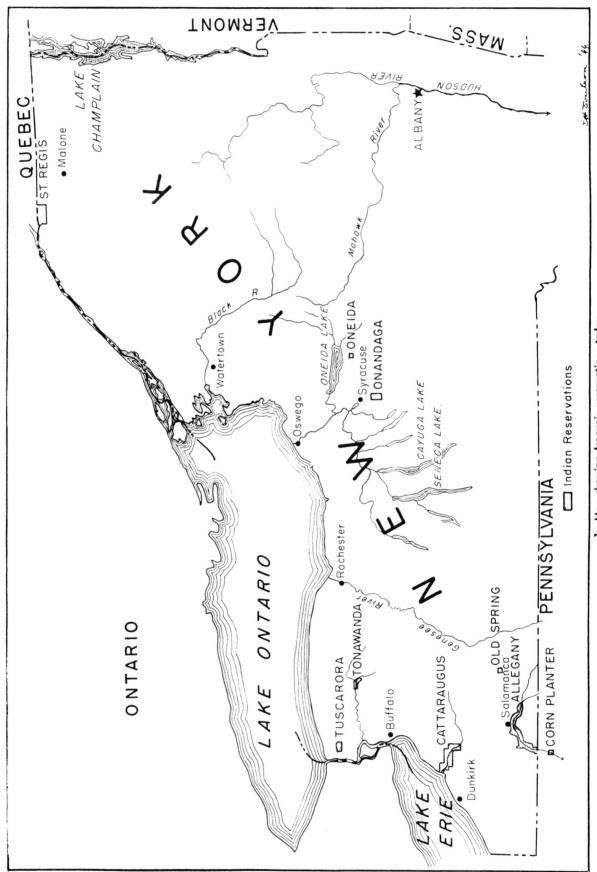

1. Map showing Iroquois reservations today.

IROQUOIS CRAFTS

BY

CARRIE A. LYFORD

Edited by Willard W. Beatty, Director of Education

UNITED STATES INDIAN SERVICE

CONTENTS

ILLUSTRATIONS

IROQUOIS DESIGNS

Illustrations through the courtesy of:

(AMNH)   American Museum of Natural History, New York City
(BAE)   Bureau of American Ethnology, Washington, D. C.
(CM)   Charles Mohr
(CNHM)   Chicago Natural History Museum, Chicago, Illinois
(MAI)   Museum of the American Indian, Heye Foundation, New York City
(NY)   New York State Museum, Albany, New York
(RM)   Rochester Museum of Arts and Sciences, Rochester, New York
(WF)   William Fenton

Line drawings of Iroquois designs were prepared by Mr. Albert van der Loo of the Construction Division, United States Indian Service.

The map of Iroquois reservations in New York State was drawn by Mr.. E. H. Coulson of the Forestry Division, United States Indian Service.

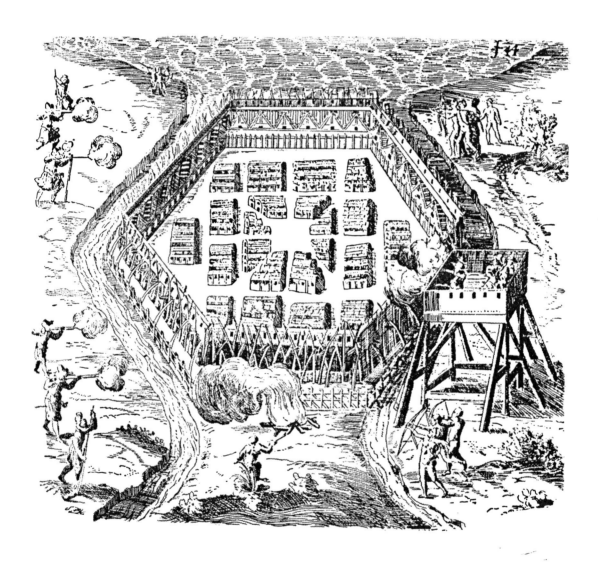

2. Onondaga palisaded village

INTRODUCTION

HISTORY OF THE IROQUOIS

Indian history on the North American continent reveals nothing more stirring and colorful than the story of the League of the Iroquois, the five (and later six) tribes or nations which, under Dekanawideh, founder and law giver, had been welded into a powerful confederacy about 1570. The tribes had been weakened by continuous wars with the Algonquin and their own kinsmen, and the League was formed for the double purpose of acquiring strength and for the establishment and enforcement of peace. The nations that formed the League were politic and judicious. They expected all other nations to acknowledge the League's supremacy and join it beneath the symbolic peace tree.

The League of the Iroquois was governed by a carefully worked out constitution that was transmitted orally from one generation to another by certain leaders (lords or sachems) whose business it was to learn and to recite the laws and regulations. For many generations these laws and regulations were recorded in a collection of wampum belts and strings, twenty-five of which are preserved today in the New York State Museum, whose director has been proclaimed "the keeper of the wampums."

In spite of the ideal of peace, the history of the League, during the seventeenth century, was one of intertribal warfare. The members of the League showed themselves fierce and formidable. They obtained firearms from the Dutch with whom they came in contact early in the century and, thus armed, they developed a power destined to make them the scourge of the Indian tribes from the Atlantic to the Mississippi and from Ottawa to Tennessee. They are known to have penetrated as far west as the Black Hills and to have attacked the Catawba in South Carolina and the Creek in Florida. The golden age of the League was from 1650 to 1755, after which its power declined. In the eighteenth century the tribal locations and movements were determined by the French and British Colonial policies in their struggle for the control of the continent.

The "Iroquois," as the members of the League were called by the French, the "Five Nations," as they were known to the English, called themselves the "men of men" or "original men." They had come to the east from west and south about 1400, and had settled in villages that extended from west of the Hudson River to the Genesee and from the Adirondacks south of the St. Lawrence to the headwaters of the Susquehanna. They represented only a portion of the linguistically related tribes that formed the Iroquoian group. Other tribes of Iroquoian stock extended up into Canada and south of the Chesapeake to the Carolinas, while outlying bands lived in Tennessee.

The five tribes or nations that made up the League included the Mohawk, who were the most easterly of the five tribes and called themselves "The possessors of the flint"; the Oneida, the "granite people" or "the people of the standing stone"; the Onondaga, the "people on the hills," who took their name from their position on the top of the hill or mountain; the Cayuga, the "people at the mucky land"; and the Seneca or "the great hill people." In 1722 the Tuscarora, "the hemp gatherers" or "the shirt wearing people" who had come up from the Carolinas, joined the confederacy,

9

and thereafter it became known as the "Six Nations."

The term "longhouse" was at one time symbolically applied to the League, and its members spoke of themselves as the "Hodinonhsio'ni o'non," "the people of the longhouse." The symbolic longhouse was represented as extending from the Hudson River to Lake Erie. It sheltered within its walls the five tribes who kept the five fires of the longhouse. At the ends of the house stood the doorkeepers, the Mohawk at the east and the Seneca at the west. In between these were the Oneida who kept the second fire and the Cayuga who kept the fourth fire. They were regarded as the younger brothers whose duty it was to care for the captives. In the center were the Onondaga who kept the ever-burning central fire and presided over the council of the league, and whose principal village (Onondaga, later Onondaga Castle) was the capital of the confederacy. At one time Onondaga was one of the most important and widely known towns in North America north of Mexico.

The Iroquois as a league did not take part in the American Revolution, but let each nation decide upon its individual action in relation to the colonies. At the close of the war those who had espoused the cause of Great Britain removed to lands in the province of Ontario assigned to them by the crown of Great Britain. About two-thirds of the descendants of the original Iroquois now live in Canada. (12,223—1940 census). Some time after the Revolution, the Iroquois remaining in this country were recognized by the United States as a nation, and the tribes were assured peaceful possession of their reservations in New York State under the treaty of Canandaigua, proclaimed in 1794, and subsequent treaties. Most of the Iroquois of the United States continue to live on the New York reservations, with the exception of the Oneida who were moved westward and finally settled near Green Bay, Wisconsin, in 1846. The 1943 census listed 3,520 Oneida in Wisconsin.

It is estimated that at the time of their greatest power the Five Nations numbered between 10 and 15 thousand. Today there are about 6,850 Iroquois living in New York on the six reservations set aside for them—Cattaraugus (Seneca, Cayuga, and Onondaga), Allegany (Seneca and Onondaga), Tonawanda (Seneca and Cayuga), Tuscarora (Tuscarora and Onondaga), Onondaga (Onondaga, Oneida and Mohawk) and St. Regis (Mohawk). Many others are scattered about the United States. The largest numbers in New York State belong to the Mohawk and Seneca tribes. A few of them continue to follow "the old way." The so-called "pagan Seneca" are often called the "longhouse people" as they still retain the longhouse which serves as a center for their ceremonies.

There are probably no full bloods among the Iroquois in the United States, as admixture with the Dutch, English, Welsh, French and other Europeans began at an early date and has continued through the centuries. Large numbers of the Iroquois left the reservations to secure an education and to gain a livelihood and are active in the world of industry and trade.

1

HABITAT

VILLAGES

The Iroquois were a hunting, fishing and agricultural people, living in compactly-built villages consisting of from 20 to 100 houses built on high, level tracts of land or on bluffs removed from streams or lakes, surrounded by small vegetable gardens, orchards, and cornfields often comprising several hundred acres.

About the period of the formation of the League (1570), the villages were enclosed by a single or double row of palisades or stockades erected to protect the inhabitants from attack by hostile tribes. The stockades were made of 15-foot logs, sharpened at one end and set in a continuous row in an earth embankment. In a description of his travels (1535) Ramusio tells of a strongly palisaded Iroquoian town known as "Hochelaga" consisting of 50 houses, each built with a frame of stout poles covered with bark. About 3,600 people inhabited the village.

The necessity of stockading the villages had almost ceased by the beginning of the seventeenth century, and by the close of the century the stockades were abandoned. Villages became less compact, but houses continued to be built near enough together to form a neighborhood.

It was sometimes necessary to change the village sites. The bark houses decayed and became infected with vermin, accessible firewood became exhausted, and the soil ceased to yield freely. Much work was involved in moving to a new site and building up a new village.

THE LONGHOUSE

The characteristic dwelling of the Iroquois was a log and bark community house known as the longhouse (ganonh'sees) designed to accommodate five, ten, or twenty families. The longhouse ranged in length from 30 to 200 feet, in width from 15 to 25 feet, and in height, at the center, from 15 to 20 feet. The average longhouse was 60 feet in length, 18 feet wide, and 18 feet high. It was built with a framework of upright posts with forked tops. The lower ends of the posts were set one foot into the ground to form a rectangular space the size of the building to be constructed. Horizontal poles were tied with withes to the vertical poles, along the sides and across the tops. A steep triangular or rounded roof was formed by bending the slender, flexible poles toward the center above the space enclosed by the poles.

The framework of logs was sheathed with bark. The bark was gathered in the spring or early summer up to mid-July. Slabs of bark 4 feet wide by 6 or 8 feet long were removed from the elm, hemlock, basswood, ash, or cedar trees. The elm bark was considered best. The bark was pressed flat under weights, and laid horizontally over the framework of poles, the slabs of bark overlapping one another like shingles. Basswood withes or strips of bast from the inner bark of basswood and hickory trees were used to fasten the pieces of bark together and to secure them to the framework. Holes for use in sewing were made in the bark by means of a bone puncher.

A series of poles, corresponding to the poles of the framework, were set up outside the bark, and close to it, on the four sides and across the roof. They were tied to the first set of poles, binding the bark firmly in place. No metal tools or commercially manufactured materials were used in the erection of the longhouse.

3. Iroquois longhouse

The longhouse had no windows. Light came from the high, wide doors at each end, and from above. A movable piece of bark or tanned hide, which could be easily tied back, was used as a door, at the entrance. In the roof were square openings to admit light and to allow for the escape of smoke. Pieces of bark were provided on the roof to close the holes when wind, rain, or snow made it necessary. They could be controlled from within by pushing with a long pole.

A central hallway from 6 to 10 feet wide ran lengthwise of the longhouse. The hallway served as a place for social visiting where children played while their elders reclined on the mats of reeds and husks provided for the purpose.

Raised 18 inches from the ground along the two sides there ran a series of compartments or booths to accommodate family groups. The booths were from 6 to 12 feet long and from 5 to 6 feet wide. They could be curtained off with skins so as to give privacy at night. Each compartment belonged to a given family and was not to be violated by members of other families. Private ownership existed, though life was carried on in a communal way. Platforms about 3 1-2 feet wide, running along the sides of the booths, provided bunks for sleeping. Small bunks were sometimes built for the children. Several layers of bark, reed mats, and soft fur robes covered the platform. About 7 feet from the ground a second platform was erected over the bunks, to be used for storage. Cooking utensils, clothes, hunting equipment, and other possessions were stowed away wherever a place could be found for them. Pits were often dug under the beds for the storage of household treasures. On the cross poles or rafters were hung large masses of dried corn (united by braiding the husks of the ears together), strips of dried pumpkin, strings of dried apples and squash, herbs, and other supplies.

At each end of the longhouse, storage booths and platforms were provided for the food that was to be kept in barrels and other large containers.

12

Down the central passage, between the booths, rough stone fire places were arranged to provide fires for comfort and for cooking, and for light at night. One house might have as many as 12 fires. Each fire place served two families. The fire built by the Indian was always a small one, not like the White camper's roaring bonfire.

During Revolutionary times the bark house of the Iroquois was fitted up with sturdy furniture. Corn husk rugs were used on the floor. Splint baskets, gourd containers, skin bags, and other handicraft products were among the furnishings. Braids of sweet grass were sometimes hung in a house to decorate and perfume it. A strong, straight bough or a thick board that had been deeply notched up one side served as a ladder to facilitate climbing to the high platform and the roof. The windows were barred with small boughs. The longhouse continued in use up to the eighteenth

4. Single family dwelling.

century after which time it was gradually abandoned. At Allegany it was used up to 1800.

SINGLE FAMILY DWELLING

During the seventeenth century a house of logs and elm bark about 20 feet long had come into use for the single family.

5. Modern Cayuga longhouse of logs.

13

About the end of the century this was supplanted by a house of white pine logs, which is still used to some extent as a place for storage. Today the home of the Iroquois duplicates that of his White neighbor of the same economic status. Small frame houses predominate on the reservations.

In the old days a small dome-shaped hut about four feet high and six feet in diameter was built of bent saplings to be used for the sweat bath in the summer time. It did not disappear until some time in the nineteenth century. Heated stones piled in the hut were covered with water poured from a bark receptacle and clouds of steam surrounded the bather, producing a cleansing sweat. The bather then was rubbed with sand, and plunged into a nearby stream.

6. Diorama showing Iroquois Indian women at work preparing 'corn.

2

FOODS

SECURING AND PREPARING

Among the Iroquois the women did the gardening; the men were the hunters. In the early days the Iroquois made much use of both fresh and dried fish and meat. The many lakes and streams of the Iroquois country yielded an abundant supply of fish during the spring fishing season. During the season of the fall hunt, long and toilsome expeditions to secure game were undertaken by the men. When times of scarcity occurred the Iroquois found it necessary to supplement the larger game by adding the meat of many of the smaller animals to the diet. In the old village sites bones have been found of bison, deer, elk, black bear, porcupine, raccoon, martin, otter, woodchuck, muskrat, beaver, skunk, weasel and dog. Domestic pigs, geese, ducks, and chickens became sources of food after their introduction into Quebec about 1620.

After the formation of the League, when the Iroquois became settled in more permanent villages, their food supply shifted more and more to an agricultural basis, and agricultural products came to form the major portion of their diet.

The entire process of planting, cultivating, harvesting, and preparing food for the family was in the hands of the women. A chief matron was elected to direct the communal fields, each woman caring for a designated portion. Certain fields were reserved to provide food for the councils and national feasts. Ceremonies were observed and special songs were sung at the time of planting and harvesting. Sacrifices of tobacco and wampum were made to the food spirits.

Through a mutual aid society, in later years known as a "bee," the women assist-

7. Seneca woman pounding corn

ed one another in their individual fields when planting, hoeing, and harvesting. They laughed and sang while they worked. Each woman brought her own hoe, pail, and spoon. When the work was over a feast was provided by the owner of the field, and everyone went home with a supply of food, usually corn soup and hominy.

Corn (maize) has always been the principal food of the Iroquois. Corn pits have been found at old village sites. Even before the formation of the League, corn, beans and squash were cultivated. Because they were grown together they were sometims called "the three sisters." The Iroquois spoke of them as "our life" or "our supporters." Considerable mythology and many ceremonies centered about them.

15

Ears of mature corn were neatly braided and hung to dry in long festoons within and without the Iroquois homes. Large quantities of corn were dried in a corn crib, built of unpainted planks in open slat construction, through which the air circulated freely. The corn crib is a characteristic feature of the small farm on the Iroquois reservations. Its use was adopted from the Indians by the early settlers.

The corn used by the Iroquois was of two common types, white dent and white flint, with occasional red ears. The white dent corn, called Tuscarora or squaw corn, was hulled or eaten on the cob, a custom adopted by the White settlers and still followed throughout the country. Flint corn was used in making hominy.

Both the green and the mature corn were used in the preparation of many popular dishes that continue in use today. Green corn was boiled on the cob, roasted on the cob in the husk, scraped and baked, scraped and fried in cakes, combined with green beans and stewed with fat meat as succotash, made in a soup when green or dried, or scraped when green and baked in a loaf.

Coarsely ground meal was made from mature corn either hulled or unhulled, pounded in a stone or wooden mortar. It was used as plain mush, combined with meat, dressed with oil, or baked as unleavened bread.

Hominy was made from the flint corn. It was prepared by soaking shelled corn in lye until the hulls could be removed. The plain hominy, hominy or hulled-corn soup in which the hulled-corn was combined with beans and pork or beef, and boiled corn bread in which the hulled corn was usually combined with beans, were popular dishes made of mature corn.

Charred corn was used the year around. Corn to be charred was selected when well along in the milky stage. The ears were set on end in a row before a long fire. Roasting proceeded until the moisture was dried from the kernels. Then the corn was shelled and further dried in the sun. The charred corn was so reduced in bulk and weight that it could be easily stored or transported. If to be kept for some time, it was cached in earthen pits. It could be preserved for several years and was used both uncooked and cooked or pounded fine and mixed with maple sugar. In the old days it was made up into cakes for the use of the hunter or warrior. In later years the charred corn has been used chiefly at ceremonial functions.

Many of the Iroquois food preparations, such as succotash and hominy, have grown popular on the American table and the names by which the Indians knew them have been added to the American vocabulary.

The cultivation and use of the several varieties of corn by the Iroquois gave rise to a need for special implements and utensils for handling the corn products. In every Iroquois home was to be found the mortar and pestle, the hulling basket, a hominy sieve basket, a netted scoop for removing ground corn from the mortar and for sifting out the coarser grains, a corn scraper, ladles, trays of bark and wood, and a long paddle for stirring corn soup and for removing the loaves from boiling water. The Mohawk used a soft hulling bag or basket in which the corn was twirled to remove the hulls after it had been boiled in lye.

Ten or more varieties of beans, varying in size, shape, and color, were cultivated by the Iroquois. Since the Iroquois did not use milk and cheese, beans were their only nitrogenous food when meat failed. The beans used were commonly known as bush beans, wampum, purple and white kidney beans, marrow-fat beans, string, cornstalk, cranberry, chestnut lima, hummingbird, white (small), wild peas, bean vines, and pole beans.

Beans were used alone to some extent but seem to have been more often combined with corn or squash when prepared for eating. Beans are still used as an ingredient in Iroquois corn bread.

16

Squashes and pumpkins, both fresh and when dried for winter use, have always been favorite foods of the Iroquois. Crook neck, hubbard, scalloped and winter squashes and hard pumpkins, artichokes and leeks, as well as corn and beans, have been cultivated by the Iroquois. Wild cucumber, turnips, and edible fungi were also used as food. Sunflower oil was used in the preparation of many dishes.

Blackberries, blueberries, checkerberries, choke cherries, wild red cherries, cranberries, currants, dewberries, elderberries, gooseberries, hackberries, hawthorns, huckleberries, June or service berries, red mulberries, small black plums, red and black raspberries, strawberries and thimble berries were all used by the Iroquois, though there is no evidence that they were cultivated. Acorns, beechnuts, butternuts, chestnuts, hazelnuts and hickory nuts were eaten. By 1779 apples, peaches, pears and cherries had been introduced from Europe. Muskmelons and watermelons were much used in later years. Fresh wild strawberries, dried blackberries, blueberries, and elderberries or huckleberries were combined with hominy and corn bread to give added color and flavor.

Maple sugar was an important article of the diet and was used almost as much as salt is today. Maple sap was used as a beverage, both fresh and fermented. Salt was little used. The sunflower was grown in quantities and its seed used for medicinal purposes.

Gourds and tobacco were cultivated by the Iroquois. The gourds were made to serve many useful purposes, as cups, dippers, spoons, and bowls in the home, and as rattles in the ceremonies and dances. Tobacco (Nicotiana rustica) was raised for both secular and sacred purposes. The Iroquois believed that tobacco was given them as a means of communication with the spiritual world. By burning it they could send up their petitions with its ascending incense to the Great Spirit and ac-

8. Collecting maple sap in birchbark container.

ceptably render their acknowledgments for his blessings. Special tobaccos were used in ceremonies. Tobacco was cast on the waters, especially on falls and rapids, to propitiate the spirits within and was put in small bags attached to masks to make them more effectve. The men and some of the women smoked tobacco mixed with sumac leaves and red willow bark.

COOKING

In the old days, fire for cooking was usually built in a sunken pit. Foods were grilled in the flames, boiled in pots of clay supported over the fire by stones or branches, or baked in hot ashes raked aside from the fire. Strips of inner bark, the ends of which were folded together and tied around with a splint, formed a primitive emergency kettle. The bark kettle was suspended be-

17

9. Clay pot

tween two sticks over a fire and filled with water, into which the meat was dropped. By the time the bark had been burned through the meat was cooked.

The making of clay pots for use in cooking must have occupied much of the time of the primitive women. The characteristic extension rim on these early Iroquois pots provided a ridge where a bark cord could be tied around the neck without slipping, so that the pot could be hung from the crotches of branches set, tripod fashion, over the fire. The rounded base made it possible for the pot to maintain an upright position when set in the fire or soft earth. With the coming of the colonists, kettles of copper, brass, and iron replaced the baked clay pots. Cook stoves have been in use on the reservations for many generations.

OBTAINING FIRE FOR COOKING

Fire was made to serve many purposes in primitive life. The Iroquois used fire to hollow canoes and mortars out of logs, to fell large trees that were to be used for buildings, and to provide heat for cooking and for other domestic uses. (See p. 56)

In pre-colonial days fire was started by friction, and the Indians had many devices by which a spark could be secured. The device characteristically used by the Iroquois was a bow and shaft or pump drill. It consisted of a weighted upright stick or

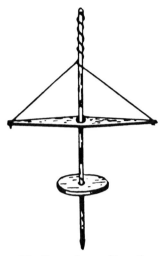

10. Pump for making fire.

spindle of resinous wood about one inch thick and 1 1-2 to 4 feet in length, to the top of which was secured a leather thong or string, the ends of which were attached to the ends of a bow that was 3 feet in length. A small wheel was set upon the lower part of the shaft to give it momentum. The base of the spindle was inserted in a notch in a piece of very dry wood, near which a piece of frayed rope (tow) or decayed wood (punk) was placed. When ready to use, the string was first coiled around the shaft by turning it with the hand. The bow was then pulled down quickly, uncoiling the string and imparting a spinning motion to the shaft, revolving it to the left. By the momentum thus given to the wheel the string was coiled up in a reverse manner and the bow was again drawn up. The bow was then pulled downward again and the revolution of the shaft reversed, uncoiling the string, and recoiling it in reverse as before. This alternate revolution of the shaft was continued until the rapid twirling of the spindle created a friction which, as it increased, ignited the powdered wood upon which it rested. The piece of tow that was placed near the point where the spindle rested on the board, took fire and quickly lighted kindling that had been placed nearby.

PRESERVATION AND STORAGE OF FOOD

The Iroquois built shelters for their farm and garden equipment and well ventilated corn cribs of unpainted planks in which corn could be dried and kept, and they dug underground pits or caches (root cellars) for the storage of corn and other foods. The pit was dug in the dry season, and the bottom and sides lined with bark. A watertight bark roof was constructed over it, and the whole thing covered with earth.

Corn, beans, berries and other fruits were dried for winter use. Braided bunches of corn were hung beside long spirals of dried squash and pumpkin, outside the log cabin or from the rafters within the cabin. Charred and dried shelled corn was kept in bark barrels which were buried in pits. Pits of well preserved charred corn have been found near ancient village sites. The bark barrels were of all sizes, with a capacity ranging from one peck to three bushels. They were made of black ash bark with the grain running around the barrel, and were stitched up the side and provided with a well-fitting bottom and lid. In addition to storing corn, the barrels were also used to store beans, dried fruits, venison and other meats, and articles of clothing and personal adornment.

Surplus meat and fish were dried, smoked, or frozen for later use. For storing the dried meat bark barrels were lined with deer skins.

19

3
CLOTHING AND ACCESSORIES

The early costumes of the Indians consisted of furs and tanned skins worn as
robes when the weather was cold. These
were gradually replaced by manufactured
materials introduced by the early travelers
and traders but buckskin clothing for working and hunting continued in use up to the
nineteenth century. There are evidences
that broadcloth was brought in by the English and French as early as 1537. After
Champlain's expedition in 1609 cloth was
more generally available. By the last
quarter of the seventeenth century broadcloth and calico had become popular for
both men's and women's garments. Graves
of that period indicate that considerable
use was made of broadcloth. It has been
preserved wherever it came into contact
with brass or copper kettles. In some cases
the color as well as the texture has been
retained. Silk had come into use by the
latter part of the eighteenth century; vel-
veteen became popular during the last quarter of the nineteenth century. Both silk
and velvet were used in decorating broadcloth garments, which had been the ac-
cepted costume of the more prosperous Iroquois since the beginning of the nineteenth
century.

The style of these early cloth garments
was similar to that of the skin garments,
but gradually garments of both skin and
broadcloth were cut after European fash-
ions, though native decorations continued
in use—trousers, jackets, and vests were
trimmed with quills, beads and fringe.

That the Iroquois prized commercial textiles is indicated by the ratification of a
treaty, November 11, 1794, in fulfillment
of which the Federal Government was to

11. Early Seneca costume.

20

12. Seneca woman with baby.

as a work board upon which to roll strips of buckskin or of vegetable fiber, an activity that occupied much of the time of the women.

Other garments, gradually added to the short buckskin skirt, included leggings, moccasins, and a deer or bear skin robe, dressed with the hair on it. The robe was finished with a fringe about the armholes and along the lower edge of the skirt. In summer the woman continued to wear only the short skirt of skin.

The costume worn by the woman just before the Revolution (1770), included a skirt of broadcloth or turkey cloth (calico), patterned after the old buckskin skirt, a

make a yearly payment of "goods" to the Six Nations. To the present day each Seneca is entitled to receive six yards of calico or twelve yards of unbleached sheeting once a year from the United States Government, which conscientiously fulfills the treaty.

WOMAN'S COSTUME

In early times the woman wore a buckskin wrapped around her body like a skirt, overlapping from the left side to the right side as a modern man's garments overlap. At the top, the buckskin skirt was folded down a few inches over a band of buckskin that was tied about the waist. This secured the skirt firmly. The left side of the skirt was on top and could be thrown back to bare the right leg so that the thigh could be used

13. Seneca woman's costume.

21

14. Woman's leggings

long jacket, over-blouse or tunic with sleeves, a flannel underskirt, leggings that came only to the knees, and a shawl usually of dark blue broadcloth, two yards square, to serve as a robe or wrap in winter. A small shawl about one yard square was used as a head covering. The shawls were often embroidered in one corner. Broadcloth was much used by those who could afford it.

Like the early skirt of skin, the skirt of the later costume was left open to the knee on the right side. The entire border and the corner on the left side were embroidered with beads or silk ribbon. Beads and ribbon were often used in combination.

The border design on the skirt usually consisted of the sky dome symbol with the celestial tree growing from the top of the sky, the branches curving out to signify life. The corner design showed the big tree of light that existed in the middle of the earth.

The jacket or over-dress showed unmistakable evidences of White contacts. Usually of light flannel or turkey cloth (calico) of solid color, green, red or blue, it was made to be loose fitting. Partially gathered at the waist, and extending half-way to the knees, it had long, full sleeves, a ruffled yoke, and it fastened up the front with silver brooches. Both the jacket and the ruffled yoke were usually finished with a narrow edging of white beadwork often combined with silk ribbon in contrasting color. The clothing of those who had wealth and position was ornamented with many rows of silver brooches.

The woman's leggings were made of bright red or dark blue broadcloth, slit up the front from four to six inches, ornamented with a narrow border of white beading and colored ribbon along the slit edge and a wider border across the bottom. A narrow bead edging finished the outer seam. The earlier leggings had been of deer skin embroidered with porcupine quill work.

Armlets, knee bands, and wrist bands of cloth or velvet, decorated with beaded designs, formed part of the ceremonial costume. Silver armlets, finger rings, hair ornaments, and ear rings were also used. A beaded scotch cap was worn by the Tuscarora and Seneca women. Handsomely beaded bags were carried with the broadcloth and velvet costumes. During the early days the Mohawk woman wore a little sack of seed corn attached to her belt but that disappeared when she ceased to wear the native costume.

After 1860 even the later costume was seldom seen except at the regular festivals, for the majority of the Iroquois women had adopted the costume of their White neighbors.

Iroquois women parted their hair in the middle. Married women wore a single braid, doubled up and tied or bound with a quilled or beaded buckskin binder. At one time elaborate bone combs were used. Unmarried women wore two braids and colored the scalp at the part. The hair was well oiled with sun flower oil or bear grease.

A red face powder, with a delicate fragrance, made from the pulverized, dry-rot of the inner portion of the pine, gave a smooth, velvety finish to the skin.

22

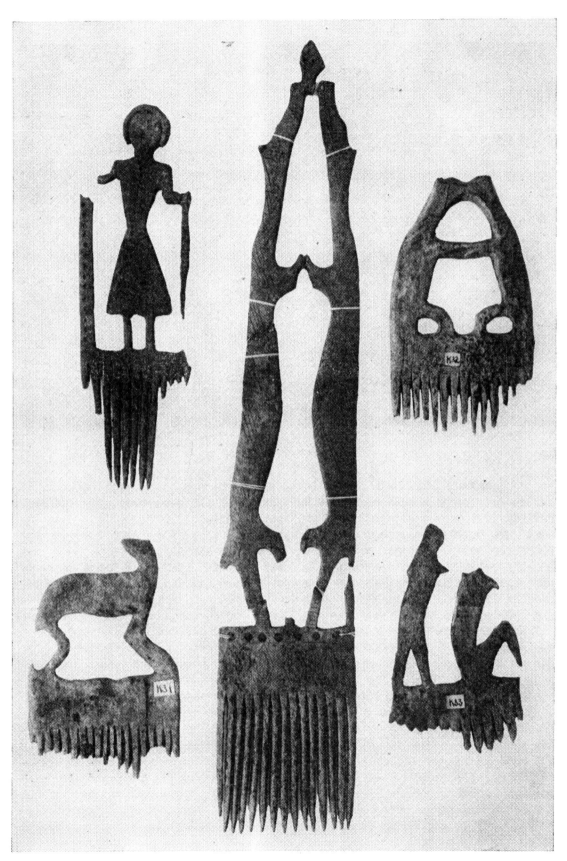

15. Iroquois combs

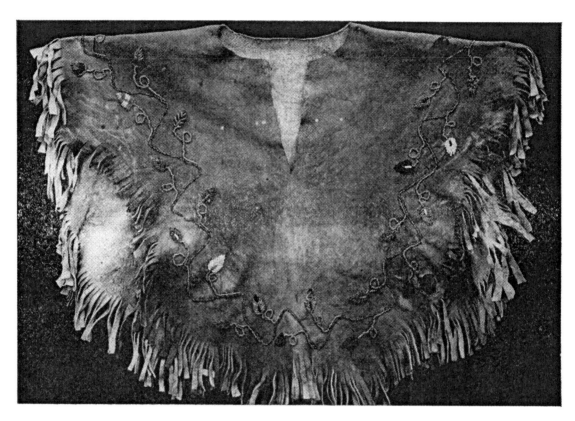

16. Mohawk buckskin shirt.

MAN'S COSTUME

When the first explorers reached this continent the Iroquois man wore only a skin breech cloth, adding a fur robe of bear skin for necessary warmth. In early historic times his costume consisted of a breech cloth, a bear or deer skin robe consisting of two skins joined at the upper corners, worn one in front and one in back, tight deer skin leggings that went above the knees, moccasins, and a turban or skull cap. The costume was often enriched by the addition of dyed hair and feathers on the head dress, fringes of ermine on the sleeves and front of the coat, and knee bands, wrist bands, arm bands, necklaces of bear claws, leg ornaments of deer hoofs, knee rattles, and ornamental belts embroidered with porcupine quills. A service belt of deer skin to which necessary possessions could be attached was wound twice around the waist and tied in front. The war club and scalping knife, worn in the front of the belt, completed the warrior's attire. Face and body painting and tattooing were practiced.

The chief wore a deer skin belt over one shoulder diagonally across the chest and tied at the left side. Both it and the service or waist belt were decorated with porcupine quills in woven or embroidered patterns. On ceremonial occasions the deer skin shoulder belt was replaced by a sash woven of native fibers or of brightly colored yarn with a long fringe at the ends. This sash was the most prized article in the costume.

The early leggings of tight fitting deer skin came up to the thigh and were provided with strips or thongs of skin to attach them to the belt that was worn around the waist. They extended to the moccasins and were fastened at the knees with garters. The leggings were decorated up the front with porcupine quill embroidery. While those worn by warriors were fringed

24

17. Iroquois man's buckskin coat.

at the outer seam, those worn in times of peace were not fringed.

The later leggings were of red or dark blue broadcloth, cut on straight lines, broad and loose fitting. The broadcloth legging was finished with a broad band of beading across the bottom and a beaded border along the seam up the front of the leg.

Early in the colonial period the Iroquois began to wear leather hunting coats and trousers cut in European fashion. The leather trousers or leggings were sometimes fringed and decorated with porcupine quills and beads. Brass buttons were used on the

18. Onondaga man's coat.

leather coats. Leather leggings and moccasins were worn to some extent until the middle of the nineteenth century (1840-1850). White shirts that hung outside the trousers were part of the later costume. Shirt fronts or vests to be worn at ceremonials were often heavily beaded with floral designs. It was in the dance that the Indian most desired to look his best, and the elaborate Iroquois costumes were prepared especially for the tribal dances.

At one time the men wore a fringed kilt of softly tanned doe skin similar in style to the kilt of the Scottish Highlander. It was fastened around the waist by a belt and hung to the knees. Quill work and ornaments were used for decorating the kilt, which was a favorite portion of the dance costume. In later years various fabrics were substituted for deer skin in making the kilt.

The breech cloth of deer skin or broad-

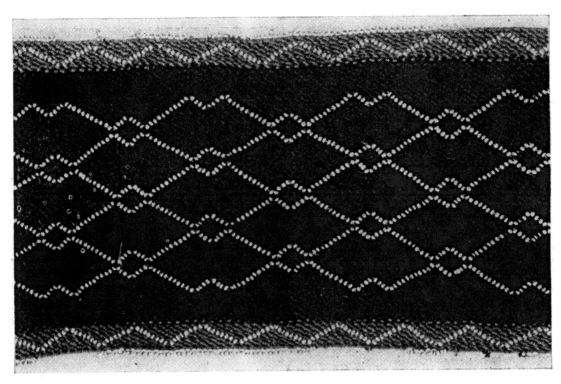

19. Woven sash with beaded design and border.

cloth was a quarter of a yard wide and two yards long. It was passed between the legs and drawn up through the belt at the front and back so that the ends hung down over the belt before and behind. A handsome design was often beaded on one or both ends of the breech cloth.

Until the middle of the nineteenth century most of the men wore long hair, divided into two braids. Warriors shaved or burned the hair, leaving only a scalp lock.

In the early days the head of an animal or the skin of a raccoon or other small animal served as head covering. At one time a round cap, woven of willow sticks, in two layers, was worn for better protection against a stroke from a war club. Later this type of helmet developed into a skull cap or round turban. It was made over a frame consisting of a band of splints shaped round to fit the head, with two cross splints arched over the top. This was covered with tanned skin, red or blue broadcloth, velvet, or a fancy silk handkerchief, and bound at the rim with a quilled, beaded, or silver band. A cluster of soft feathers was fastened to the top of the cap with a single long eagle plume, set in the tip of the crown, and inclining backward. The eagle feather was set loosely in a cup-like contrivance so that it twirled or quivered with every motion of the wearer or with the slightest breeze. This feather was the distinctive feature of the Iroquois cap. On the warpath, the men

20. Man's beaded hat.

27

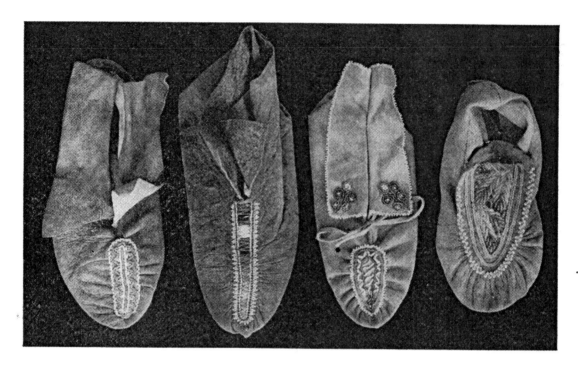

Moccasins: Oneida, Iroquois, Iroquois, Onondaga.

wore a head roach like that of the Ojibwa[1], made of hair from the deer's tail.

In the early part of the nineteenth century some of the men and even some of the women wore the tall beaver or "plug" hats then fashionable among the Whites. On the tall crown of the hat they placed band after band of silver, according to their financial means.

A necklace of sweet grass was worn with the historic costume by both sexes. It was made up of the fragrant marsh grass, braided into three-strand cords. Every three or four inches it was decorated with small disks of sweet grass. These were sometimes ornamented with bead work in simple designs. The disks resembled the old stone runtees. Fourteen of them were customarily used on a neck piece.

MOCCASINS

The Iroquois wore soft-soled buckskin moccasins of two types. The moccasin of the Cayuga and the Seneca was made of one piece of skin with a seam at the heel and

[1]Ojibwa Crafts (Chippewa), U. S. Indian Service. Handcraft Pamphlet No. 5. Haskell Institute, Lawrence, Kansas.

over the top of the foot, but the bottom was seamless. At the back, a quarter of an inch was lapped over from each side giving added strength to the seam. The seam up the front of the moccasin was gathered, with notches cut out between the gathers so that the two sides could be brought closely together. After the seam had been made the gathers were beaten or pounded so that they would lie flat. The gathered seam was often covered with a narrow strip of quill or bead work. In some cases fine bead work was done directly on the moccasin at the sides of the seam. The thread used in sewing was of sinew. The needle was made of a small bone taken from near the ankle joint of the deer, and was known as the "moccasin needle."

The Mohawk in the eastern part of New York made a moccasin of different type, similar to the moccasin of the Algonquin, in which the toe of the moccasin was gathered unto a U-shaped vamp that was sometimes decorated. In some cases a separate piece of the same shape as the vamp was

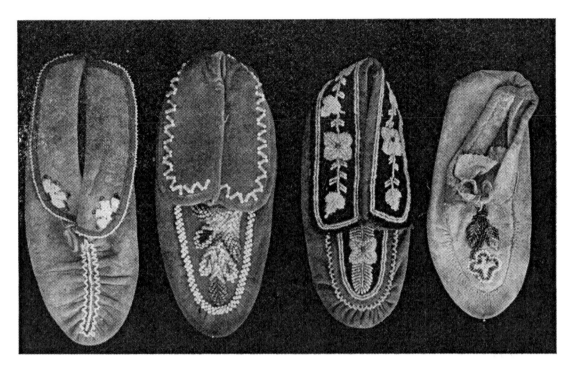

22. Moccasins: Seneca, Seneca, Seneca, Mohawk.

elaborately embroidered with quills or beads and tacked over it. These decorative vamps were removed from worn moccasins and used on newly made ones.

The Iroquois moccasin extended several inches above the ankle and was fastened with deer skin thongs drawn through holes on each side. Usually the top of the moccasin was turned down to form a cuff. In the moccasin worn by the woman this cuff was all in one piece. In the man's moccasin the cuff was separated at the back seam so that the two sides spread apart.

The cuffs of the Iroquois moccasins were decorated at different periods with embroidery of moose hair bristles, woven and embroidered porcupine quill work, bead embroidery, or ribbon work as the different materials became available. A pair of old Seneca moccasins shows porcupine quills, fine beads, and silk ribbon work all used together. Small metal disks, and cotton and silk braids were used with the bead designs in moccasin decoration. The cuffs of the early moccasins were sometimes fin-

ished by fringing the edge of the skin, by adding a fringe of moose hair bristles, or with a plaited quill border.

Velvet and broadcloth cuffs were popular on the later moccasins. Both black and brown velvet and red and black flannel were used for cuffs. The edges of the velvet cuffs were bound with cotton cloth or cotton braid or with silk ribbon. An old pair of Tuscarora moccasins shows black velvet cuffs bound in red woolen braid.

The moose hair embroidery on moccasins was worked out in delicate scroll and floral patterns. Porcupine quills were used in scrolls, in interlaced zigzags, and in fine floral patterns. Bead embroidery patterns ranged from very fine triangles, scrolls and double curve designs on the Seneca and Cayuga moccasins to heavy floral designs on the Tuscarora and Mohawk moccasins. Opaque, translucent, and transparent beads in many different sizes were used in moccasin decoration at different periods.

At one time the Iroquois made moccasins of braided or twined corn husks or basswood fiber.

29

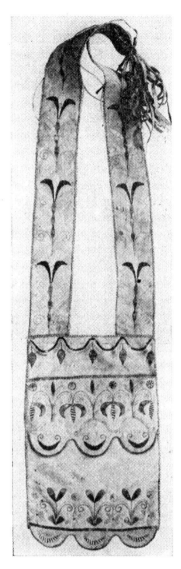

23. Quilled bag.

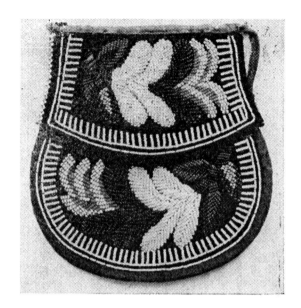

24. Embossed beading on bag.

BAGS

At different stages of their culture the Iroquois made bags of fur, bags woven of vegetable fiber, and bags elaborately beaded with a cloth or tanned skin background.

The entire skin (with the head and tail left on) of the white weasel, mink, squirrel, fawn, or marten was made into a bag to serve as a knapsack or a tobacco pouch. As a knapsack the bag was filled with food for an expedition and hung to the girdle of the warrior or hunter. The small tobacco bag or "fire bag" was made for carrying the short-stemmed pipe. Similar bags were in constant use in the home for holding cherished articles.

Bags of tanned skin served as containers for strings of wampum. They were about six inches deep and eight inches wide, usually slightly narrower at the top, laced up the sides with a strip of skin, and finished with a three or four-inch flap at the top and a four or five-inch fringe at the bottom. Leather strings were provided for carrying.

Flat, rectangular carrying bags, about nine by twelve inches, were made of basswood fibre, in both close and open weaves. (See Ojibwa Crafts).

From the middle of the eighteenth century through the early half of the nineteenth century (1750-1850), small, flat beaded bags made of commercial cloth and fashioned after the prevailing style of side bag worn on the belt by the White women of the period, were popular. The bags resembled a soldier's wallet. They were about six by six inches and almost hexagonal in shape, but were usually curved across the lower edge and had a flap falling over from the top. Many of them were decorated with rows of fine beads in several colors, some of the rows separated by a beaded zigzag

30

25. Seneca leggings; Iroquois sash.

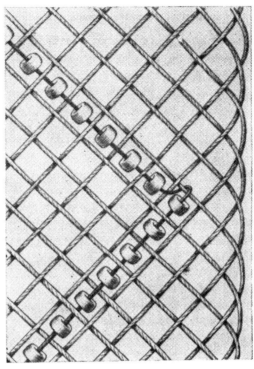

26. Detail of weaving.

pattern that closely resembled rickrack. Others were embroidered with bead designs in which the double curve pattern was used. Silk ribbon was often inserted between rows of beads to give color. Beaded belts were sometimes made to wear with the bags. These elaborately beaded articles were often finished with cotton lining and binding.

About 1860 a new type of heavily embossed embroidery done with opaque white glass beads appeared on bags and other articles made by the Tuscarora and the Mohawk. The coming of tourists to Niagara created a demand for souvenirs. Bags, pin cushions, and needle cases were made in many shapes and were heavily embroidered with bird and flag designs. Large translucent beads were much in vogue. Beaded strings ending in metal jinglets filled with dyed horse hair were sometimes used as a finish around the edge of a bag. The decoration was heavy and inappropriate, rendering the articles useless for their intended purposes.

27. Belts: Iroquois, Onondaga.

WOVEN YARN SASHES

Bright-colored wools brought from Europe were woven by the Indians into ornamental sashes similar to those worn by the French voyageurs in the eighteenth century. The technique employed in making the sashes was a method of finger weaving done without loom, heddle, bobbin, or shuttle. One hundred and forty or more strands were frequently used. Narrow garters were woven in the same way with as few as forty strands. Two or more of the narrow strips were sometimes stitched together overhand to form a broad sash, ten inches or more in width.

The Iroquois in common with the western Woodland Indians, enriched the woven sashes by the addition of white beads, which were carried on a special thread, and were woven in so as to outline the zigzag, diamond, and hexagonal designs. The sharp pointed zigzag design suggests lightning and arrow points. The V and W designs predominated in the narrow sashes. Beads were also worked into the deep yarn fringes (20 inches to one yard in length) at both ends of the sash, producing an elaborate article.

Many of the sashes were made of one color. Red was used in most of the sashes. Two shades of blue, sage green, a rich shade of old gold, and white were also used. As many as five colors appear in some sashes. Red sashes four or five inches wide sometimes had a border of dark green or other color, three-fourths of an inch wide on each side, with white beads woven into the border as well as into the body of the sash.

A fine, close weave was sometimes used in making the sashes. With a tightly spun commercial wool this produced a sash of firm texture. Other sashes were loosely woven and soft. In one collection a black sash in which a zigzag pattern was worked out in white beads is dated 1741.

Cheap, machine-made imitations of the old sashes have been numerous, but they can easily be distinguished from the hand-made finger-woven sashes of the Iroquois. The old Indian weave has been so little practiced during recent years that it has almost died out. (See Ojibwa Crafts).

4

SECRET SOCIETIES AND CEREMONIES

The tribal organization and national identity of each of the Six Nations has been retained by conservative groups through the years in large measure because of the existence in each tribe of secret societies, the most generally known of which are the "Secret Medicine Society" and the "False-face Company." These societies are of ancient origin, and their rituals, in which dreams have played an important role, apparently have been transmitted with little change for many years, especially among the Seneca who have preserved them with great fidelity. The societies varied in the different tribes. In the early days it was not permissible to recite the rituals or chant the songs to any one who had not been initiated, so the societies were but little understood until a comparatively recent date.

THE SECRET MEDICINE SOCIETY

The ceremonies of the Secret Medicine Society were usually developed as festivals of thanksgiving, each one of which was appropriately named. The seven chief thanks-

28. Diorama showing carving of falseface

giving festivals began with the mid-winter or New Year Festival and included "Thanks to the Maple" or "Sap Dance" at the beginning of spring; the "Planting Festival" or "Seed Dance" (Soaking of the Seeds) in May when the dogwood was in bloom; the "Berry Festival" or "Strawberry Dance," a first-fruits thanksgiving when the strawberries ripened; the "Green Bean Festival" or "String Bean Dance" when the string beans ripened; the "Green Corn Festival" or "Ingathering of Food" at mid-year; and the "Harvest Festival" or "Bread Dance" in October to return thanks for a bountiful harvest.

Much time was spent in preparation for and observance of the ceremonials. Costumes, rattles, drums, canes, and other articles considered appropriate for each ceremony and thanksgiving festival were assembled. Though the festivals were of a religious nature there was feasting and great merriment during the afternoon and evening when both religious and social dances were held. Enjoyment of life was considered a phase of thanksgiving. After the ceremonial offices had been performed, the days were devoted to athletic contests between the tribes.

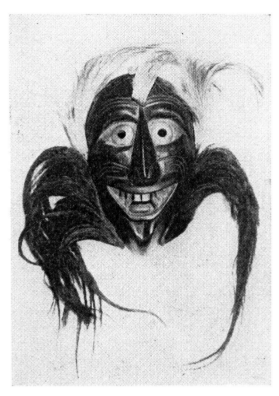

29. False face, Laughing Beggar.

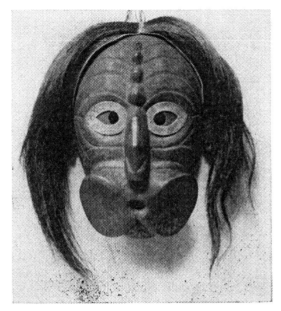

30. False face, Red Spoon Mouth.

FALSEFACE COMPANY

The falseface ceremonies of the Iroquois were held for the purpose of exorcising evil spirits and driving away diseases. In the late fall and spring members of the society went from house to house, wearing masks and trying to behave like persons whom the masks represented. Rattles of horn, of wood splints, and of hickory bark or snapping turtle shells were carried.

Highly colored wooden masks depicting mythological and legendary characters, with wry, hideous mouths, are known to have been used by the Seneca as far back as the seventeenth century.

There were many types of masks representing different characters and serving different purposes. Corn husk masks were used by the Huskface Society and masks of buckskin were made to impersonate cannibal clowns who kidnapped naughty children. Masks designed to be worn by mem-

bers of the Falseface Society were likenesses or symbols of supernatural beings.

According to ancient tradition a strange creature in the form of a great head with terrible flaming eyes made his home on a huge rock over which his long hair streamed. During storms the howling of the wind was thought to be his voice. Another tradition told of several bodiless spirits with ugly visages that had the power to inflict ailments and send disease among people. Still a third tradition told of two brother heads, one in red, the other in black, and a cousin, one-half red and one-half black. It was these traditional figures that suggested the use of the falseface masks. Representations of the bear, the pig and other animals are also seen in the old masks.

Carved Masks. The carving of wooden masks was a ceremonial procedure and was usually carried on by artists of exceptional ability. Masks varied according to the style of the artist who carved them. To give it potency and to keep within it the spirit of the tree, a mask was carved on the trunk of a living tree, usually the basswood, willow, cucumber, or other tree of soft wood. A three days' ceremony preceded the carv-

31. Woven Iroquois corn husk mask.

32. Braided Iroquois corn husk mask.

ing. Sacred tobacco was burned, a pinch at a time, as a plea for forgiveness to the Tree Spirit for the necessity of mutilating the tree. The tobacco smoke was blown into the roots and among the branches. Because of this offering of tobacco, it was thought the tree would not die, and the scars left on the tree would heal over in from two or four years. Today masks are often carved on barn beams.

After the mask had been roughly blocked out, the entire block was cut off the tree, the features carefully carved in high relief, the eyes encircled with wide rings of sheet metal, and the entire face usually painted black or red in solid color. A mask painted half red and half black was known as the whirlwind mask, as it had the power to divert an approaching storm. For this reason it was hung on trees facing the wind. "If he had sought his tree in the morning, the artist painted the mask red, but if he found the tree and commenced carving after noon

the mask would be black." (Fenton) Unpainted masks were worn by clowns.

Long strands of horse hair, either black or white, or of basswood, moosewood, or slippery elm, were fastened to the top of the mask and hung down like hair on both sides to the knees. Tiny medicine bags were often attached to the masks to make them more efficacious.

Masks about five by seven inches were made for children. Miniature masks from one to three inches in diameter, made of stone, wood, or corn husks, were attached to the larger masks, hung from the end of the leader's pole, or were used as charms to protect buildings from witchcraft. At one time the small mask was sent as a notification of election to candidates for admission to the Falseface Society.

Corn Husk Masks. The members of the Huskface Society, made up chiefly of water doctors, wore corn husk masks originally made of braided strips of corn husks sewed together in grotesque representation of a human face. In making the later corn husk masks, on the Alleghany reservation, a twined technique was used. Often the face was partially covered with a husk fringe and closely resembled a husk mat in appearance. The face was sometimes carved of wood and surrounded by a thick, corn husk fringe for hair.

To make a braided corn husk mask, three strips of tightly braided corn husks were coiled round and round with a center hole left in each coil—in one coil for the mouth, in the other two coils for the eyes. The coils were then sewed together with husk fiber or twine to form the face. A nose, shaped from a piece of corn husk, was added to complete the face.

A twined corn husk mask was made by twining two weft fibers around warp fibers back and forth across the face of the mask, leaving openings for the eyes, nostrils and mouth.

The masks were finished by the addition of eyebrows and a binding of braided or knotted husks, the loose ends of which were left to represent hair.

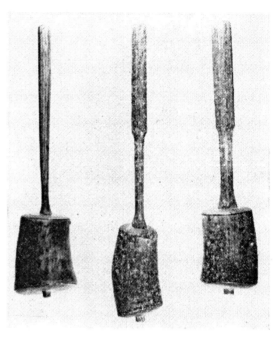

34. Seneca horn rattles.

The husk faces were worn at the midwinter ceremony where the husk maskers acted as spirits of the harvest and appeared with digging sticks and hoes, performing a weird dance to inaugurate the new year. The masks were also used in the society's ceremonials at the time of the green corn dance in the spring and whenever help was given to someone in need, so that the identity of the donor would not be disclosed. An elaborately carved cane was often carried by the masker. Among the Iroquois, agricultural emblems signified fertility, and as the corn husk masks related to the harvest they were made by the women. The wooden masks were carved by the men.

DANCE CUSTOMS

The Iroquois have had many dances, most of them associated with ceremonial observances. Some of the dances were performed by selected dancers, attired in full costume and painted for the occasion. In other dances both men and women participated.

The War Dance, interspersed with patriotic speeches and witticisms, and the Feather Dance, consecrated to the worship of the

33. Water drum.

36

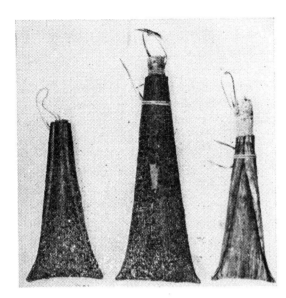

35. Seneca bark rattles.

Instrumental music and singing played an important part in the dances. The singers were seated in the center of the room and the dancers passed around them. The instruments used to mark time for the dances and songs included turtle shells rattles, tiny gourd or squash rattles, deer hoof rattles, feather wands, rhythm sticks, flageolets or ceremonial whistles and the water drum.

Flageolet. A primitive whistle was made from the wing bone of a large bird. The later flageolet or flute resembles a clarinet. Its Indian name signifies "blow pipe." It was usually made of red cedar and is about eighteen inches in length, and a little over an inch in diameter. The finger holes, six in number, are equi-distant but are nearer one end than the other. Between them and the mouth piece, which is at the far end, is the whistle, which is much like a common whistle. It makes six consecutive notes from the lowest, on a rising scale. The seventh note cannot be sounded, but the three or four next above can be made. This is the whole compass of the instrument. As played by the Indians, the flute affords a sort of wild and plaintive music. It is claimed as an Indian invention.

Great Spirit, were the most popular dances. They were performed by a selected group of fifteen to thirty dancers who had distinguished themselves by their activity and powers of endurance.

There were other ceremonial dances known by the name of the society by which they were performed, as for example the Falseface, Eagle, Bear, or Buffalo, or by the name of clan animals such as duck, fish, and pigeon. The dances were held in the longhouse or upon a suitable green.

36. Seneca turtle rattle.

37

Water Drum. The bark water drum, used for ceremonial occasions, was from six to twelve inches in diameter and from three and one-half to seven inches high. It was usually made of a cedar or basswood log carefully hollowed out to form a mere shell. Two pieces of bark were sometimes shaped to form the drum. The bottom was made water tight with a perfectly-fitting cross section of a log carefully secured with spruce gum. Over the top, a piece of raw hide was tightly stretched and held firmly in place by an encircling rope of grapevine or vegetable fiber. A small hole was made in the side near the bottom of the drum and fitted with a stopper or bung. When in use the drum was filled about one-third full of water. When the water was at different levels the drum gave off different tones. The drum sticks were very small and sometimes ornately carved.

Rattles. The turtle shell rattle was made by removing the body of the animal from the shell, replacing it with a handful of flint corn or cherry stones, then sewing up the opening. When it was to be used in the feather dance, designs were painted on the underside of the turtle shell. The neck of the turtle stretched over a corn stalk or short stick often served as a handle. The hollow shell of a squash, filled with corn, was also used as a rattle. The sound varied according to the size of the squash. As many as twenty rattles, all of different tone, were sometimes used at one time.

After the dances were over, such favorite foods as hulled corn soup and corn bread boiled with kidney beans were served by the feast-makers and either eaten on the spot or carried home in the receptacles with which each person came provided.

5

GAMES AND SPORTS

BALL GAMES

The Iroquois enjoyed games and sports, in many of which they acquired remarkable skill. Games were associated with their religious ceremonies, for it was believed that they were pleasing to the Great Spirit and they were often performed with religious intent. During a famine or epidemic a game might be ordered by the medicine men to propitiate the spirits. At the concluson of their sacred observances the groups remained together to enjoy a period of sport and festivity. In the early days competitive games were entered into with nation playing against nation, village against village, or tribal division against tribal division. They were not carried on for individual glory. The prize was victory.

Field days with exhibitions of strength and skill added much to the pleasure of Iroquois life.

Ball play, hoop games, and target shooting were popular summer sports. Ball play has always been among the favorite games of the Indians. The most popular ball games among the Iroquois were lacrosse, shinny, and double ball, the last two being played by the girls and women. Foot races were always enjoyed and long periods of practice usually preceded them. In winter, snow shoe races, shinny, ice ball, and snow snake and snow boat were enjoyed. Indoor games of chance played in winter made use of cherry stones, peach and persimmon stones, sections of deer bones, carved wooden tallies and other hand made equipment.

The men put much labor into the carefully prepared snow shoes, snow snakes, spears, javelins, lacrosse sticks, tallies, and other articles used in playing the games.

Double-ball. Double-ball was a woman's game. To play double-ball, two small buckskin bags were filled with sand and fastened together with a leather thong from one to two yards in length. A large group could play the game. Each player held a crooked stick with which the balls were tossed from player to player in an endeavor to get them over the goal lines. The players were grouped in two teams and could intercept each other, catching the bags on their sticks and passing them on to their own goal line.

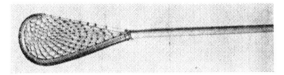

37. Seneca lacrosse bat.

Lacrosse. Lacrosse was played by the American Indians centuries before the discovery of America. It was described by a French trader in 1662-1669 and by a missionary at an even earlier date. In ancient times a wooden ball, made from a burl or knot of wood, was used. Later a small ball of deer skin, stuffed hard with moss or hair and sewed up with sinew, came into use. The original bat had a solid, curving head. Later a racket with a curved end, across which a net of sinew or deer skin thongs was strung to a point far up the handle, was substituted for the bat. These rackets were sometimes carved. Because of its resemblance to a bishop's crozier the racket was called "la crosse" by the early French colonists and the game came to be known as "lacrosse."

When the game was to be played a large field or sheet of ice was cleared and "gates," consisting of two poles ten feet high, were erected about sixty yards apart at opposite ends of the field to serve as goals.

Before the game began each player removed all clothing except his breech cloth. The teams, of six or eight men each, assembled at each end and endeavored to direct the ball with a racket into the opponent's goal, knocking it on the ground or in the air, or carrying it in the net on the racket. The game was carried on with much enthusiasm and lasted usually from noon until evening. Sometimes the contest was so close it was necessary to finish it on another day.

Shinny. Shinny was popular among the Iroquois women. It was played with a flattened buckskin ball, the opposite sides of which were painted in different colors. Each player, of which the number was unlimited, held a stick, three or four feet in length, curved at one end. Sometimes the stick was painted or carved. The ball was driven by the stick only; the hand could not be used.

Two poles to serve as goals were set up about three feet apart at opposite ends of the field which was two hundred or more yards long. The participants were grouped in two opposing teams. The object of the game was for each team to drive the ball through the goal of the other team. To play, the ball was placed in a shallow pit in the center of the field by the umpire while the teams lined up just inside the goal posts. At a signal both teams or chosen members of each side rushed to the hole in an endeavor to secure the ball and drive it toward the opponent's goal.

GAMES OF CHANCE

Like other Indians the Iroquois were fond of games of chance and had a great variety of them. For each there were special pieces of equipment and special rules. Dice games were played with wild plum or peach stones and cherry pits, beans, deer and elk horn or bone buttons, and carved wooden tally sticks or counters.

Peach Stone Game. (Also known as Dish Game). Peach stones were filed or cut down to an oval shape so that they looked like smoothed-off hickory nuts. One side was slightly burned to blacken it. The game was played by placing six of the peach stones, all with the same color up, in a flat bottom earthen or wooden dish carved out of a knot or burl of a tree, sometimes decorated with carving. The bowl was then shaken violently and brought down on a pile of skins with a whack. The count was based upon the number of pieces of each color exposed. If all of one color were up the count was ten, all but one of the colors up counted five, and two of a color up counted two. The counters were red beans. An equal number of beans were given each side and the game was played until one side had won all the beans. Sometimes it took as long as four days or more to play a game.

The peach stone game was played three times a year in the longhouse—at the Indian New Year, the Maple Sugar Thanksgiving Festival, and the Green Corn Festival in September.

Deer Button Game. The deer button game was played by two or more with eight buttons, an inch in diameter, carved out of deer bone and blackened on one side. They were cupped in the hands and thrown down, usually on a blanket. The relative number of black and white faces turned up determined the count. If they all turned up white, the count was twenty; if seven of the eight turned up white it counted four; if six turned up it counted two. The game continued until one player had won a bank of fifty beans. Sometimes the buttons were decorated with dots and with circular and radiating designs.

Ring, or Cup, and Pin Game. The ring, or cup, and pin game enjoyed by many Indian tribes was played with seven conical bones loosely strung on a leather thong, about eight inches in length. The bones were usually smaller at one end and could be slipped into each other. At one end of the thong was a small piece of fur and at the other a hickory stick three and one-half

inches long. The game was played by holding the stick in the hand, swinging the bones upward, and trying to insert the pointed end of the stick into one or more of the bones as they were descending. Each bone had a value of its own, the highest value being on the lowest bone, and the one who could total up the highest score was the winner.

HOOP GAMES

Hoop games were played with shooting sticks, poles, spears and javelins. Hoops of different sizes were made of a bent, unpeeled sapling, usually of hickory or maple, tied around the overlapping ends with bark. Some of the hoops were filled with an elaborate hexagonal weaving. Spears varied in size from small darts to poles fifteen feet long.

Hoop and Javelin Game. The javelin was five or six feet in length and three-fourths of an inch in diameter and was usually made of hickory or maple. It was sharpened at one end, finished with care and striped spirally. The hoop was eight inches in diameter and left open or filled with a netting. Sometimes the javelin was thrown horizontally by placing a fore finger at its end and supporting it with thumb and second finger; in other cases it was held in the center and thrown with the hand raised above the shoulder.

Fifteen to thirty players with three to six javelins apiece were arranged on each of two sides, according to tribal divisions. The javelins were the forfeit, and the game was gained by the party which won them. A line was mapped out on which the hoop was to be rolled and the two bands of players were stationed on opposite sides at designated distances from it. The hoop was rolled on the line by one party in front of the other and the javelins were thrown. The players who failed, handed their javelins over to the other side.

The side which threw the greatest number of javelins through the hoop as it rolled, won the game.

Hoop and Dart Game. The hoop and dart game was played with a hoop, made of a sapling, and darts four or five feet in length, of which each player usually had two.

The players lined up on two sides about ten feet apart. A member of one party threw the hoop so that it went spinning along the ground at a rapid rate and the others launched their darts at it. The object was to stop the hoop as it rolled by, impaling it. If a player missed, his dart was forfeited, but if it went under the hoop, he retained it.

Hoop and Pole Game. The hoop and pole game was played with a hoop made of an unpeeled bent sapling tied with bark, sixteen inches in diameter, and six poles, seven feet in length. Five or six persons played. The hoop was rolled and all threw their poles. The one whose pole stopped the ring owned it. The others then shot in turn, and the owner of the hoop took all of the poles that missed it, and shot them at the hoop, winning those that he put through it. If two men stopped the hoop, they divided the poles.

Snow Snake. Snow snake, which may be called the national game of the Iroquois, is still a popular winter sport. Snow snakes were smooth, polished, flexible rods made from various kinds of hard wood (maple, walnut, or hickory). They were from five to nine feet in length and one inch in diameter at the head, tapering to about half an inch at the tail. A slight notch was made near the small end, or the upper surface was left slightly concave near the end to allow for a better finger hold. The head was rounded and turned up slightly on the under side like the fore part of a skate runner. Today the head is pointed with lead to help its balance. The snow snake was made with precision and given a fine finish.

When there had been an abundant snow, a smooth, shallow course was laid out on a level stretch, sometimes slightly down grade, by pulling a smooth-barked log from ten to eighteen inches in diameter in a straight line through the track for from 90 to 120 rods. This packed the snow, making a trough 10 to 18 inches deep. Any protruding objects were removed. The course was then sprinkled with water to form an ice crust.

When the game was to be played those taking part gathered at one end of the track and in turn threw the "snakes" with force, skill, and accuracy so as to make them travel the longest distance possible in the shortest time. Before it was thrown the snake was rubbed with a skin saturated with some secret "medicine" (oil or wax). The player grasped the snake firmly in the right hand placing the forefinger in the notch that had been cut in the snake tail and, balancing it with the left hand, stooped toward the ground with the snake held horizontally over the rut in the snow. Then with a few quick, short steps he threw the snake with considerable force along the rut. The snake travelled with the speed of an arrow sometimes for the distance of 60 or 80 rods. A goal-marker indicated where each snake stopped. Victory was declared when the player or team had sent four or more sticks over the greatest distance in a specified number of trials.

Target Shooting. Target shooting was carried on with a bow from three and one-half to four feet long. It had a difficult spring which could scarcely be bent by an inexperienced person and the arrow was shot out with great force. The arrows were three feet long, feathered at the small end with a twist to make them revolve in flight. Every man had his arrows marked so that he could identify them. Originally the arrows were pointed with a piece of flint, horn, bone, or chert (rockflint) which made them exceedingly dangerous missiles, penetrating deeply any object which they hit.

Throwing the Arrow. Throwing the arrow was a game requiring swiftness and muscles. The person who threw the greatest number of single arrows into the air before the first one thrown fell to the ground won.

41

6
ANCIENT CRAFTS OF THE IROQUOIS

The five nations that later formed the League of the Iroquois were an active, busy people, skillfully preparing all that was needed to meet the vigorous conditions of forest life before the coming of the White man. Refuse heaps in New York State have yielded to the archaelogist many evidences of the industry of the Iroquois and their predecessors in articles of stone, clay, antler, bone, and other substances that have withstood the years. Existing collections of native Indian handicrafts show carefully made pieces of early pottery and beautifully carved utensils of wood that testify to the skill that had been attained in these arts in prehistoric times. Almost nothing remains of the prehistoric weaving, braiding, and embroidery, developed on the more perishable materials, so that there is little on which to base a study of the purely native techniques and designs in these media.

In 1609 the Dutch found the Iroquois manufacturing net, twine, and rope from elm, cedar, and basswood barks; weaving ceremonial baskets, mats, dolls, moccasins, masks, belts, and burden straps from vegetable fibers and buffalo hair; embroidering skins with quills, moose hair, shells and native beads; fashioning clay vessels and clay pipes; making dishes and spoons of bark; carving ladles, spoons, masks, and bows and arrows; cultivating maize, beans, squashes, and tobacco; and making an unleavened bread of corn. Many of these activities ceased after contact with White settlers. Others have persisted. The making of the unleavened bread has continued to the present time.

In the old days the Iroquois men were busy hunting, fishing, and waging war. They built the longhouses and the palisades, made the canoes and paddles, mortars and pestles, snow shoes, lacrosse sticks, war clubs, pipes, bark and wooden dishes, and other wooden implements. They also carved the ceremonial spoons and paddles and the ritualistic wooden masks. Usually the men helped to gather the materials for handicraft work and assisted the women in clearing the land and harvesting the crops, though in the early days they felt a disdain for field work. As there grew to be less necessity for activity in war and on the hunt the men assisted more and more with farm work and the handicrafts.

The Iroquois women made the ropes and cords of elm and basswood bark, fashioned the clothing, made baskets, sieves, and pottery vessels, did the weaving and embroidery, carried on the agricultural work, gathered firewood, roots, berries, fruit, and nuts, smoked and dried the fish and game, carried the burdens on the expeditions, and tanned the hides with the help of the men.

With the coming of the traders, the industries and domestic life of the New York Indians were revolutionized. The production of certain handicrafts was stimulated through the introduction of manufactured beads, yarns, colored silks and broadcloths, knives, needles, and other metal tools with which to carry on their work. The making of some native craft articles ceased altogether. Pottery died out. Skins ceased to be used for clothing. Contact with the Europeans came so early in the settlement of the continent that by the beginning of the nineteenth century much of the skill in

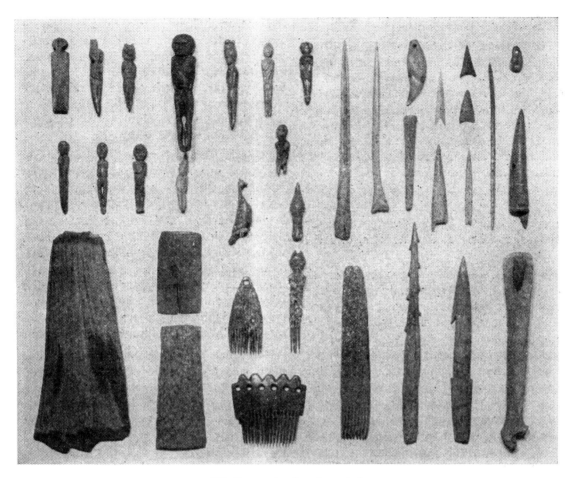

38. Bonework of early period.

native craft work had been lost. The Iroquois arts and crafts, as we know them, show European influence in form and design though to a considerable extent the techniques used have continued to be based on techniques that were developed in prehistoric times.

Fortunately, from well illustrated descriptions in the New York State Museum Bulletins, from the Annual Reports of the Royal Ontario Museum of Archaeology, and from museum specimens, much can be learned of the past life of the Iroquois and of their activities during the latter half of the nineteenth century. Based on the information contained in these reports a revival of ancient handicraft work known as The Indian Arts Project was carried on for several years (1935-1941) on the Tonawanda and Cattaraugus Reservations. Sponsored, and financed in large part, by the Rochester Museum of Arts and Sciences, it was operated as a relief measure under the Temporary Emergency Relief Administration and the Federal Arts Project. With the help of old craft workers on the reservation who knew some of the old techniques authentic copies were made of Iroquois implements, household articles, ceremonial objects and wearing apparel. Work was carried on in birchbark, wood, clay, silver, buckskin, wool, and broadcloth and with porcupine quills and beads. Old crafts such as finger weaving, tanning, carving, pottery making, quill embroidery and bead weaving were revived. The articles produced have served to acquaint the present generation with the crafts of the earlier Iroquois.

43

USE OF ANTLERS, STONES, BONES

Their domestic life and the agricultural activities in which the Iroquois had engaged from pre-Columbian days created need for a variety of implements which were cleverly devised from antlers, stone, bone, shell, and wood. Decorative designs were incised on many of the shell, antler, and bone articles and carved on the wood implements with knives of chert (rockflint).

Implements. Antlers were used for both tools and ornaments such as knife handles, digging blades, awls, punches, combs, wedges, spoons, bodkins, needles, and fish hooks.

Primitive stone adzes and axes (celts) in various shapes, sizes, and weights were used in working with charred wood when excavating canoes, mortars, and other containers. Stone mortars were used for pounding corn, grinding mineral paint, and for pulverizing roots and barks for medicine. Rounded cobblestones were used for mullers or pounders. Some of the stone mortars were so small that they could easily be carried in a basket. Axes, banner stones, bone blades, grinding stones, stone gouges, hammerstones, and notched stone sinkers are found in great numbers in old Iroquoian sites.

The Iroquois excelled in the manufacture of bone instruments. The bones of many animals and birds were applied to some useful purpose, notably bones of the deer, elk, moose, bear, buffalo, duck, turkey, goose, and the heron and other large water birds. Awls, long, narrow knives, gouges, arrow points, fish hooks, harpoons, needles, shuttles, and many other objects were made from bones. The flat shoulder blade of a deer, or a tortoise shell, sharpened upon a stone and fastened to a short stick, made a hoe.

Decorative Articles. Many smaller bones were used for decorative purposes, serving as beads to form necklaces. Perforated and polished bone beads have been found by the hundreds.

Bone combs, made as early as the seventeenth century, are in a fair state of preservation, though the teeth are often broken. At first the combs were simple in design with only a few strong teeth. Many of the more recent combs have been carved to show figures of men, birds and animals and are decorated with line designs.

Weapons. The men of the Five Nations devised a number of weapons effective in aggressive warfare, which they fashioned with much skill. The making of spears, bows and arrows, and the tomahawk or war club occupied much of their time. Such weapons were constantly being broken, lost, or worn out and had to be replaced so that a steady industry was carried on. But the great preponderance of implements found on the old village sites are those that were made for industry and hunting, not for war.

Spear heads or spear points found on Iroquoian sites of great antiquity reveal the hand of a master craftsman in their delicate chipping, symmetry, and beautiful notching. They are among the most beautiful specimens of the chipper's art. The spearheads vary in their size, shape, and notching. They are larger than arrowheads. Spears were fastened to the ends of shafts or handles and were used in warfare, hunting, fishing, and at ceremonials.

The arrowhead or arrow point was probably of later origin than the spear and is thought to have been evolved from it. Arrowheads were made of varieties of stones, chert, yellow jasper, quartz, hornstone, diabase, argillite, chalcedony, and slate. They varied in size and shape and showed all the colors that nature produces. The greatest number of Iroquois arrowheads were triangular, delicately chipped from chert. Except for a few long, slender types, arrowheads were usually less than one and one-half inches in length.

Bows and arrows were kept in sheaths or quivers woven of corn husks, or made of bark, or of skin decorated with quill designs.

Wooden shields were made and used in

44

39. Iroquois war club.

the early days as a protection against spears and arrows.

The Iroquois war club was originally a heavy weapon two feet in length made of ironwood with a globular head five or six inches in diameter. The head sometimes resembled a human face or a ball enclosed by claws. War clubs were also made with a fine piece of flint, bone, or stone attached to the end, or a deer horn inserted in the edge. Through trade with the Colonists, brass, steel, and iron war clubs replaced the wooden ones. Though no longer used in warfare, the war club has continued to have a place in ceremonial observances.

The tomahawk, which the Iroquois could throw with great dexterity, was originally a stone weapon somewhat like an ax, with a deep groove cut around the outside by means of which the wooden handle was firmly attached with a willow withe or rawhide thong. Sometimes the tomahawk was gaily painted and adorned with beadwork, feathers, fur and hair.

USE OF SHELLS

Shells were used by the Iroquois for both useful and ornamental purposes. Because of their thin, sharp edges they made good implements for cutting, scraping, and digging. Their concave shape made them useful as containers (cups, spoons, and bowls) and their delicate coloring and attractive texture gave them value for personal adornment and other decorative purposes.

Beads and Runtees. When the Dutch reached Manhattan in 1609 they found the coastal Algonquian slowly and laboriously making large quantities of disk shaped (discoidal) and cylindical beads from small, fresh water, spiral shells (Columbella mercatoria), perforating them through the center, and stringing them on threads of deer sinew or bark. With their steel instruments the Dutch soon developed improved methods of making beads and other shell ornaments and sold them to the Indians in great numbers. The Indians purchased steel drills for their own use and the native production of shell articles was vastly increased.

Small discoidal, spherical, and cylindrical shell beads have been found in great abundance in excavated sites which were occupied about 1650. Beads and ornamental disks or runtees of shell have also been found in graves of the late seventeenth and early eighteenth centuries. The runtees are large ornaments of shell, most of which are decorated with incised or picked-in designs. (See p. 69)

Shell beads for decorative purposes were gradually replaced by imported glass beads. Not many shell beads have been found on sites later than 1800. After this period the use of shell beads was chiefly in the wampum strings and belts used in councils and for ceremonial purposes.

Wampum. Of the beads that were manufactured and used by the Iroquois those known as "wampum" are by far the most significant. Though the term wampum has been used in some places to include both the discoidal and the cylindrical beads, the true wampum is an Indian-made shell bead, cylindical in form, averaging about one-quarter of an inch in length by an eighth of an inch in diameter, perfectly straight on the sides, with a hole running through it the long way. Some of the wampum beads prepared for commercial trade were as long as half an inch but none of the long beads has been found in the wampum belts. Wampum was made from the quahaug or hard shell clam (Venus Mercenaria) which provides both white and purple beads. The central axis (columellae) of the great conch shell (pyrula Carica), was used for white wampum.

Colored wampum had a special significance for the Iroquois. Colors ranged from a pale pink and delicate lavender to a

40. Loom for weaving wampum belts.

deep purple. The purple beads were generally known as black wampum and were especially prized for political purposes. White was the emblem of purity and faith. Both pink and white wampum were appropriate to peace.

The first use of wampum was probably for personal adornment. Wampum beads were used in necklaces, collars, head bands and armlets and were sewed on articles of clothing.

Up to 1693 the Iroquois also used wampum as money, either in strings or loose. It served as currency between the Indians and the Dutch and English colonists. Enormous quantities were used to pay the tribute demanded from the Iroquois by other Indian tribes.

The Iroquois strung wampum on cords for use in minor tribal transactions and wove it into belts to convey messages, record treaty stipulations, carry on condolence ceremonies and for other religious and social purposes.

Wampum is mentioned in the legends of the Iroquois, many stories having been told of a wampum bird with which the legendary hero Hiawatha seems to have had an obscure connection.

Wampum Strings or Strands. Both the discoidal beads and the cylindrical or true wampum beads were strung on nettle fibers or sinew to form wampum strings, several of which were usually tied together at one end in a bunch, bundle, or sheaf. Sometimes a special color arrangement was observed in stringing the wampum in order to convey an inter-tribal message or to serve as a record in some minor tribal transaction. A string of invitation wampum was provided with small sticks or wooden handles at the ends, so notched as to indicate the number of days before the event. A wampum string was sometimes bestowed by the clan matron when announcing the permanent name of an adult.

Wampum Belts. Probably nothing which the Iroquois made has been of such universal interest as the wampum belts used as seals of friendship when their treaties were ratified. It was said that "the Whites should never regard an Indian Council as serious, or regard it as a dangerous thing unless the national wampums were brought forth and displayed."

Wampum belts were woven of cylindrical beads with a special technique on long strands of sinew, leather, vegetable fiber,

46

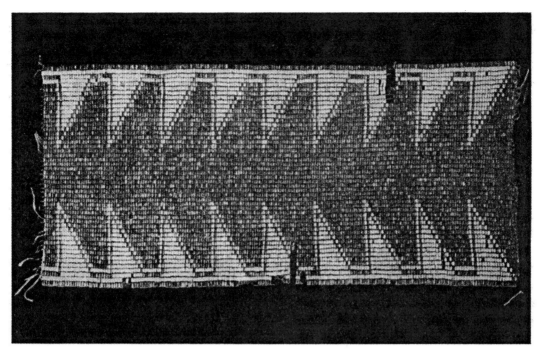

41. Wampum belt with "Evergrowing Tree" design.

or string. The various vegetable fibers on which wampum was strung included slippery elm (Ulmus fulva) fiber, dogbane (Apocynum cannabinum. L.) or black "Indian hemp" sometimes called amyroot, swamp milkweed (Asclepias incarnata), and the hairy milkweed (A. pulchra) also called white "Indian hemp," toad flax (Linaria linaria), and Indian mallow (Abutilon-avicennae) popularly known as velvet leaf.

When the belt was to be made, both ends of the strands were put through holes in a small piece of deer skin so spaced as to keep the strands at equal distances from one another in parallel lines. The extreme ends of the strands were then fastened to the ends of a piece of splint which had been sprung as a bow, and the strands were thereby held in tension to serve as the warp. The beads that were to form the width of the belt were then strung on a weft thread (in the early days the weft thread was of sinew) which was passed under the fiber strands so that one bead was lengthwise between each two strands, at right angles to them. The thread was then passed back along the upper side of the strands and again through

each bead so that it was firmly held in place by means of two threads, one passing over, and the other under the strands. When the belt had reached the desired length the ends of the warp and weft strands were tied and the ends of the belt finished off, usually with a leather fringe. The belt varied from 5 or 6 beads in width to as many as 50. The finished belts were usually from four to six inches wide and from one foot to six feet long. Old belts contain 1980 beads, on the average. There are 3000 beads in the William Penn belt. An old Onondaga belt contains nearly 10,000 beads.

Designs woven in the belts included hollow squares, hexagons, diamonds, overlapping triangles, crosses, diagonal lines or bars, circles, hearts, pipes, houses, and human and animal figures. The designs were arranged in symbolic patterns. Their meaning was given by the maker of the belt or was said to have been "talked into it" when a treaty was made. Thus stories told by the designs served as reminders of tribal events. The belts were shown on regular ceremonial occasions and the significance of the designs explained, a ceremony known as

47

"reading of the archives."

Some of the wampum belts were made only for temporary use, after which they were dismantled. Important belts were preserved and were entrusted to a hereditary keeper, versed in their interpretation, and thus their significance was retained.

The oldest wampum belt, known as the Hiawatha belt, is thought to date back to almost the middle of the sixteenth century when it served to record the formation of the League of the Iroquois (1570). With twenty-four other choice old belts the Hiawatha belt is today preserved in the State Museum at Albany, New York.

The Hiawatha belt was made up with a pattern showing four hollow squares outlined in white and one white, heart-shaped design in the center, all connected about midway by white lines. These designs represent the five nations with the great peace lodged in the heart. When reversed, the figure representing the heart assumes the appearance of a tree—the Great Tree of Light under which the nations meet in council. The white of the lines and the central heart are emblems of the peace, love, charity, and equity that surrounds and guards the Five Nations.

The Washington Covenant belt used during the presidency of George Washington as a covenant of peace between the 13 original colonies and the Six Nations of the Iroquois, shows symbolic figures of 15 men with outstretched arms and clasped hands extending along its length. In the center is the figure of a house. The two figures on each side of the house are the Keepers of the East and West Doors, the 13 figures clasping hands are the original colonies. The designs are woven in the dark or purple beads on a solid white beaded field which denotes peace and friendship.

The widest belt known, called the Wing or Dust Fan of Council President, shows a series of ten connecting purple, hexagon-shaped figures on a white background. Both the figures and background are edged with a white and a purple line of beads. The design is said to represent "The Evergrowing Tree" which by its repetition symbolizes the permanence and continuous growth of the Great League of the Iroquois. It was displayed whenever the League constitution was recited, to protect the Council and to keep the eyes of the 50 civil rulers free from dust.

Another wide belt, sometimes called the Presidentia, is made up with a design of overlapping purple triangles with a chain of 14 white, open diamond-shaped figures along the central axis. The background is of white beads. At one time the belt was longer and there were 16 diamonds. The chain of diamonds represented a covenant, or a chain of friendship, always to be kept bright.

On an old wampum belt, known as the General Eli S. Parker belt, there are five dark purple, open hexagons outlined in white beads. Each hexagon symbolized the council of one of the nations of the League. The white beads were emblematic of purity, peace, and integrity. The dark purple beads symbolized royalty, dignity, and determination. This belt was originally known as the "five council fires" or "death belt" of the Five Iroquois Nations and was long held by the Seneca Nation which guarded the west door of the Iroquois League or Confederacy. It signified death or war against some nation or nations and was sent from one tribe of the Confederacy to another when war was pending.

USE OF CLAY

Pottery appeared among the Iroquois with agriculture during the late pre-Columbian period. At the beginning of the eighteenth century pottery-making was skillfully carried on and widely distributed. The early pottery was strong and fine, resembling the pottery of the related Cherokee which was still carried on at a much later date. When White contacts increased, pottery began to deteriorate and was soon replaced by large iron and brass kettles from Europe.

42. Clay pipes.

Pottery jars. In the early days cooking was done in clay pots. Pots were also filled with food for the departed to use while traveling to the realm of the Great Spirit. They were placed near the sites of burial where many have since been found.

Clay pots were necessarily limited in size, ranging in capacity from two quarts to several gallons. Many of the smaller pots have been preserved, but very few of the larger ones have been found. (See p.18)

The typical Iroquois clay pot had a globular body with a rounded bottom, a narrow or constricted neck, and a projecting rim or collar ornamented with incised or carved triangular designs. A border of elongated notches that sometimes produces raised points ran around the lower edge of the collar. In some cases the collar disappeared, the neck was short, and the top rim was notched, indented, knobbed, or scal-

loped. Most of the pottery was the color of the fired clay but some of it was black and could take on a high glaze or polish.

The pottery of the Iroquois was made by the coiling process. Carefully selected clay was powdered and then mixed with a tempering material such as pulverized quartz, stone, shell, or sand to prevent cracking. It was then moistened and beaten or kneaded like bread dough. The prepared clay was rolled into ropes which were kept moist. The clay ropes were coiled upon a saucer-like base, then worked into the desired shape by continuing the coiling process. The ropes were sometimes coiled around a gourd, which insured a symmetrical form and provided a natural handle which was a convenience during the coiling process. The gourd could be rotated round and round to make the inside smooth. It could not be removed after the neck of the pot was formed

49

so was left in until it burned away during the firing process. The clay ropes or coils were patted and pressed together with a wet paddle or smoothing stone that was first dipped in water. A collar, sometimes round, but more often four-sided with an upward turn at each corner, was then formed and fitted to the neck. Line decorations were used on the collar. Triangular plots of parallel lines were incised or drawn in the clay, the direction of the lines being changed in each adjoining plot. Impressions of fingernails, corn cobs, and a cord-wrapped stick were used as decoration. Human faces and figures were used in decoration for nearly fifty years in the late sixteenth and early seventeenth centuries. Figures were often drawn at the corners of the neck or rim with three round dots punched in to represent the eyes and nose of a conventional human face. The body of the pot was usually kept smooth.

After the pot had been shaped and decorated it was thoroughly dried and baked in hot coals, entirely covered in order to avoid drafts which might cause breakage.

Pipes. The Iroquois men took high rank as pipe makers in prehistoric times, excelling both in the number and quality of pipes which they made. The early Iroquois clay pipes were the basis of the clay pipes used by the Whites. Later Iroquois pipes show much of European influence.

The Iroquois pipes were of three kinds—the pipe of elbow type with the stone bowl to be used on separate stems of reed or cane, the pipe of stalagma, with a straight stem at right angles to the bowl, and the clay pipe with the bowl and stem in one.

The early stone pipes were both numerous and beautiful. The finest pipes were those of clay, with a curved or trumpet-shaped stem and an open bowl in effigy form. The figures on the bowls represented human beings, animals, or birds.

The holes in the clay pipe stems were usually made with a willow twig which served as the core and burned away as the pipe was baked.

The pipe handles or stems were short, hence the beaded pipe bag carried by the Iroquois was smaller than that used by the Sioux and other western Indians.

USE OF BARK

The Iroquois fashioned many implements and utensils out of bark of the elm, hickory, oak and birch trees. Elm bark was most generally used. Storage barrels, pails, quivers, bowls of all sizes, trays, rattles, troughs for maple sap, traps, canoes, and toboggans were all made of bark. Sections of the elm tree with the bark left on were used for lining springs where drinking water was secured and for lining and covering caches where vegetables and fruits were stored. The Iroquois knew that the bark was ready to peel when the sap was well up in the elm trees and the leaves were the size of a squirrel's ears.

When a large piece of bark was to be removed from a tree an incision was made through the bark around the tree near the roots and a like incision was made about seven feet higher up the tree. These two horizontal incisions were then joined by a

43. Iroquois elm bark vessel.

50

vertical cut. In order to reach the upper edge of a long strip of bark it was often necessary to build a rude scaffolding against the tree. Beginning at the edge of the vertical cut, the bark on each side was loosened from the wood by use of a tapering wedge that was gradually worked in all around until the large sheet of bark came off entire. This thick bark could be divided into thin sheets by peeling it off layer by layer. If the bark was removed without injuring the sap layer the tree would continue to grow and a new layer of bark would be formed.

Containers. The inner bark of the red elm or black ash was used to make a bark barrel. The bark was shaped in cylindrical form, with the grain running around. It was overlapped and stitched firmly up the side. A bottom was fitted and stitched on and a lid attached. The barrel was used for storing dried vegetables, fruits, and seeds, and also for clothing.

A heavier barrel for the storage of grain was made from a section of the elm tree by hollowing out an upright log of desired length with the bark left on.

45. Seneca bark tray.

44. Iroquois elm bark ladle.

A bark sap tub, for the storing of maple syrup, was made from a strip of elm bark about three feet in length and two feet wide. Beginning at the point where the bark was to be turned up to give it the proper shape, the rough outer bark was removed from the two ends but it was left on the bottom and sides. The ends were then turned up and gathered in small folds at the top and tied around with a splint or fiber.

To make a bark tray for holding corn meal, mixing corn bread, and other purposes, a strip of bark of the required dimensions was prepared by rounding it at the ends, removing the rough outer surface from the ends, and turning up the ends and sides to form a shallow container. The sides were strengthened by adding splints

51

46. Maple sugar utensils.

of hickory both inside and outside of the rim and stitching them over and over with bark fibers. The interior of the old bark tray became very smooth with use.

Canoes. The Iroquois made canoes of the bark of the oak and the red elm. The bark of the oak was considered more lasting. After the rough outside had been removed from large slabs of bark they were smoothed and soaked, then stitched to a frame of ash or hickory with basswood fiber or splints. Narrow strips of ash to serve as ribs were set across the bottom of the canoe, about a foot apart. The edge of these ribs were turned up and secured under the rim of the canoe. At each end the canoe was finished with a vertical prow. Iroquois canoes varied in size from twelve feet, to carry two men, up to forty feet with capacity for thirty men. In the early days the bark canoe was extensively used in the fur trade (See Ojibwa Crafts).

Rope Making. The Iroquois made thread, twine, and woven burden straps from the fibers of the inner bark of the basswood (Tilia americana L.), the moose wood or leather wood (Dirca Palustris L.), and the

slippery elm (Ulmus fulva Michx.). Indian hemp or Dogbane (Apocynum—Cannabinum and androsaemifolium L.), nettle fibers (La porte canadensis L.), and milkweed fibers (Asclepias syriaca L.) were also used in Iroquois weaving. Basswood fiber was especially valuable for rope and for the heavier burden belts.

Bark that was to be used for thread was usually gathered in the spring when the sap was running. The outer surface of the bark was removed, then the inner bark was peeled off in narrow strips six or eight feet in length, loosely braided, and tied in bunches until needed for use. It was then boiled and pounded to render it pliable. It was sometimes necessary to repeat this process three times. Then it was washed thoroughly and dried in the sun. After it was dried the strips of bark were separated into the natural fibers running with the grain. Many of the fibers ran the entire length of the strips of bark and were often several feet in length. When separated the fibers were usually neatly braided into skeins and laid aside until needed for use as thread or twine.

52

47. Uses made of tump lines.

In addition to many other uses twine was made into nets for use in fishing. When netting was to be done, all the strands were caught at one end so that they ran lengthwise. Then each strand in turn was twisted or knotted with the neighboring strands on either side to form meshes of uniform size producing an open, elastic fiber. The work was done with a wooden needle and was often carried on by the old men of the tribe. Wild hemp was the favorite thread for fish nets but the inner bark of the mulberry, elm and basswood were also used.

The Burden Strap or Tump Line.

Before the coming of the White settlers, the Iroquois were using Indian hemp and bark fibers from the elm, basswood, and cedar to weave or braid the long straps that were used for carrying burdens. The straps were variously known as burden straps, tump lines, pack straps, and carrying straps. Slippery elm fibers made burden straps of the best quality, being finer, stronger, and more pliable than basswood fibers. Basswood fibers were good for very heavy straps. The fibers were prepared by boiling, stripping, rubbing and twisting into cords.

The burden strap consisted of a woven belt about two feet long and two and one-half inches wide with narrower tying strips at each end, usually woven all in one piece. In making the belt a twined weave was used, two weft-strands of fine fiber being twined over one another between two coarser warp strands. The weaving was started in the middle of the belt which narrowed in width near the ends. The remaining length of the warp strands were then braided to form the tie-strings for the packs. On some straps the tying strips were reinforced by braiding strips of tanned deer hide with the fiber. The tie-strings usually extended about seven feet from each end of the belt. The finished strap was fifteen feet or more in length and three or four inches wide.

Few burden straps have been made since 1820. An old craft worker on the Seneca reservation who knew how to make them taught the technique to others during the recent revival of the native arts.

Though made for use, the belt of the burden strap was often elaborated by the development of geometric designs in the weaving. A ribbed appearance was obtained by using a finer cross thread. Hairs of the moose, buffalo, deer, and elk were com-

53

48. Tump line with moosehair decoration (197 inches long).

bined with the vegetable fibers to work out decorative patterns. Porcupine quills were also used in the designs. Both the hairs and the quills were dyed to give more color to the burden straps. Rhomboid figures with a narrow white border were often used against an alternate red and blue background. In straps of a late period beads were sometimes used in the border.

On some of the finest burden straps a type of false embroidery was developed. The false embroidery was worked in during the weaving by winding moose hair, undyed or in various colors, around the woof threads so as to form a design and to add to the beauty of the finished strap. Soft tufts of white hair four inches long, from between the shoulder and rump of the moose, were dyed red, blue, and yellow for this purpose.

When in use, the ends of the finished burden strap were attached to the burden basket, baby carrier, or other burden that was to be carried on the back. The broad center of the strap was carried across the woman's forehead or chest which bore much of the weight of the burden.

Litter Basket or Burden Frame. The litter basket or burden frame was an ancient contrivance used by the Iroquois to assist in carrying burdens. Game, cooking utensils, wood, bark, and other small articles could be carried in this frame. Such frames were necessary in every home for the use of the

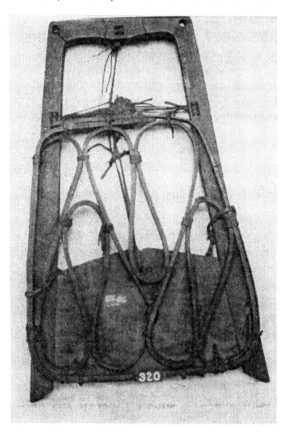

49. Seneca pack frame.

54

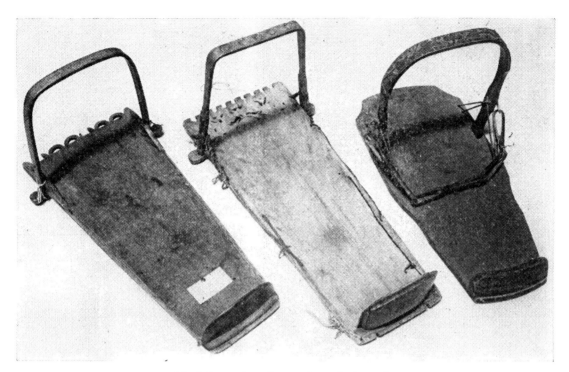

50. Baby carriers: Seneca, Iroquois, Iroquois.

home maker, the traveler, and the hunter. The frame usually consisted of two plain sticks of hickory or ash, bent in half circular shape, brought together at right angles and fastened to each other by means of an eye and a wooden head. Sometimes they were elaborately carved and finished. The upright part of the frame was the same as the horizontal except that it was longer. Strips from the inner bark of the basswood were passed between the bows both lengthwise and crosswise, and fastened to the rim to strengthen and hold it in shape. A burden strap was attached to the frame at the points where the strip of bark passed across the upright bow from side to side, and from thence diagonally across to the horizontal part of the frame, to the point where the lower strip of bark crossed that part of the frame. Several feet of rope were left at each end to attach to the burdens to be carried. After being loaded the frame was placed upon the individual's back and the burden strap was passed over the head and carried across the chest.

USE OF WOOD

Skillfully prepared wooden articles, both plain and carved, were used by the Iroquois in their domestic life and in their religious ceremonies. Before the introduction of metal tools from Europe it had been necessary to char the wood and scrape off the burned sections with stone or shell tools in order to get the forms desired. Canoes and large mortars were hollowed out of heavy logs with fire. Woodwork became easier when metal tools were introduced in the seventeenth century. It reached its height in the eighteenth and early nineteenth centuries. Mortars and wooden dishes more than a century old have been collected.

The Iroquois men were notable for their skill in wood carving. Wooden utensils were decorated with figures of animals, birds, and reptiles, usually depicting clan designs and personal totems. Designs representing human figures were used to a great extent by the Iroquois.

Bowls were made of beach, basswood, and maple. Soft curly maple knots were hol-

55

51. Felling a tree by burning and scraping.

lowed out with primitive bone, shell, or stone tools and given a high polish by continual scouring and absorption of grease, which produced an attractive lustre.

Cups of hard maple or other wood were made for individual use. The base was rounded, never flat, as the cup was always set on the ground where a small hollow could be made. An animal figure or other design was often carved on the handle of the cup. All Indians in the northern woodlands used these cups. Warriors tied them to their belts when traveling. Small wooden dishes and spoons were made for the children.

Baby Carriers. The baby carrier (cradle board, baby board, baby cradle, or baby frame) was a convenience devised by the Indian mother for carrying the baby. The Iroquois made a baby carrier on a flat board about two feet long and fourteen inches wide with a perpendicular bow near the top and a foot board at the other end, both of which were often elaborately carved. The bow, which was an inch or more wide, was braced to stand upright over the board a few inches from the top edge and was held in place by means of a cross piece passing under the board, into which the ends of the bow were inserted. Over the bow a blanket, piece of netting, or other covering was drawn to protect the face of the child. A burden strap, attached to the back of the cradle board, was carried around the forehead of the mother or across the shoulders, so that she could support the baby on her back when transporting it from place to place.

A baby carrier made of elm bark is said to be an older type than the wooden cradles. An early emergency baby carrier was made of fine twigs woven compactly in much the same form that was used in making the later wooden baby carrier.

An Onondaga baby carrier that bears the date of 1750 has a carved foot-board and bow with an openwork pattern. Sometimes the decorations included inlays of silver

and woods of different colors. About 1840 the back of the cradle board was painted with elaborate floral designs. These highly decorated cradle boards are thought to have been the work of European craftsmen or of Indians trained by them. They were especially popular among the Mohawk Indians on the St. Regis Reservation.

The cradle board when used was further elaborated by the addition of a covering or spread, usually of red broadcloth, embroidered with beads and silver ornaments, and with one or more broadcloth bands embroidered with beads. Deer skin strings were run along the outer edges of the board, and under these, bands to hold the baby in place were passed from side to side over the body of the child. Rattles, for the amusement of the baby, often hung from the bow of the cradle.

In the Indian home a baby hammock is often made with a rope and blanket. The rope is stretched between two points from four to eight feet apart and back again. The blanket is folded to give the proper length for the baby's body and to allow for three times the desired width. The center of the blanket is then passed under the ropes in such a way that one third of the blanket can be folded over the ropes from each side to the other giving three thicknesses to the cradle bottom. Usually two sticks, a trifle shorter than the desired width of the hammock, are placed between the ropes at each end of the blanket.

Baskets. The Iroquois made a great variety of baskets to serve a diversity of useful purposes. The baskets made by the various groups and individuals show some minor differences but certain fundamental techniques were employed in common by all the basket makers of the six tribes.

The Iroquois women were the basket makers, but the men helped in the preliminary heavy work of preparing the splints and in carving the handles. In a few cases the men excelled as basket weavers.

The Iroquois baskets were made with a

52. Allegany hominy sifter with hexagonal plaiting.

simple weave to serve a utilitarian purpose. They do not compare in intricacy of technique and perfection of workmanship with the choice baskets of the far Western tribes.

Elm bark, corn husks, flags, sweet grass, and black ash splints were used in Iroquois basket making.

The simplest baskets were the bark containers, boxes, and trays made of sheets of elm (Ulmus Americana) bark. They were not made in as great quantities nor were they as much elaborated as were the birch bark containers of the Ojibwa and other tribes of the Central Woodlands area. (See Ojibwa Crafts.) The Iroquois bark containers are described in the section under the heading "Articles Made of Bark."

Corn husks and flags or cattails (Typha latifolia) were made into baskets by processes of braiding, twining, and plaiting that are no longer practiced.

Sweet grass (Hierocloe Odorata) was made into baskets by a coiled technique.

(See Ojibwa Crafts).

Black ash (Flaxinus Nigra L.) splints were plaited in checkered, wicker, twilled or diagonal and hexagonal techniques to make heavy pack, utility, and storage baskets and hampers with and without handles and covers.[1]

Thin splints of the black ash were secured by hammering a small ash log to loosen the annual rings or layers, pulling the layers off in thin sheets, and cutting them into narrow strips of even width. Some of the splints were dyed before being used, to add color to the baskets.

Basket Techniques. The checkered plaiting is a simple over-one-under-one weave with two elements that are similar though they may vary in width.

The wicker plaiting is done with a more or less rigid warp and a flexible weft using the

1 Lismer, Marjorie, Seneca Splint Basketry, Indian Service Handcraft Pamphlet No. 4. Haskell Institute, Lawrence, Kansas.

53. Corn washing basket of black ash showing twill weaving.

same over-one-under-one weave.

The diagonal or twilled plaiting is also the simple over-and-under weave but the weft is carried over and under two warps, and in each row the plaiting begins one strand in advance of the plaiting in the previous row so that a diagonal effect is produced in the weave.

Hexagonal plaiting used in making trays and shallow baskets is done with three elements so arranged as to form an equilateral triangle. The splints in each set go over and under alternately each splint in the other two sets. The members of one element all pass over the members of the second and under all members of the third group of elements.

A hulling or washing basket about 18 inches deep and 18 inches across the top was made with twilled plaiting, the sides tightly woven and the bottom formed with an open sieve-like weave. It was made both

with and without handles. Two open spaces were sometimes left in the weave near the top on opposite sides to provide places in which to insert the hands to carry the basket. On other baskets, raised loops and bail handles were provided.

A shallow sifting basket used in the preparation of corn meal, and for sifting ashes and hominy was made of hickory splints with a twilled, open plaiting. Shallow rectangular baskets, 13 by 26 inches, were made for drying berries and to serve as bread bowls. A deep basket with flexible sides was made for use as a washing basket.

Basket making was given an impetus by the White trade as a demand arose for containers to serve an increased number of purposes. Bottle shaped baskets, women's sewing baskets, laundry hampers, cake baskets with lids, and other baskets that could be used in the homes of the settlers were in demand.

59

About 1860 women's work baskets were varied in some cases by twisting a few of the splints at regular intervals as the plaiting was progressing to produce a series of sharp pointed rolls or curls. Because of these projecting curls this technique came to be known by the descriptive term "porcupine work," although porcupine quills were not used in making these baskets.

Among the implements used by the Iroquois in basket making was a splint cutter, consisting of a piece of metal with several points equi-distant from one another, inserted in a wooden handle which was frequently carved. The sharp metal points of the splint cutter, when run down the length of a thin sheet of wood, cut it into splints of equal width for use in basket making.

The pack or carrying baskets, woven with wicker plaiting, were used for gathering corn, collecting firewood, carrying provisions, and even for transporting small children from place to place. When corn was being gathered the basket was attached to a burden strap which was passed around the head or the chest of the worker and the ears of corn were thrown over the shoulder into it as they were picked.

A deep basket with open weave was made for use when fishing. Planting baskets were made with compartments for different seeds, and in use were tied to the waist, leaving the hands free to drop seeds and with a hoe to cover the seeds with earth.

Designs were worked out in the black ash baskets by varying the width and color of the splints, by varying the weave, and by giving the baskets different shapes. The splints were colored with vegetable dyes or painted before using.

The Oneidas, who excelled in splint basketry, made a basket of black ash splints in two widths, using the checkered plaiting and decorating the wide splints on the sides with a border of dots or a geometric or leaf design. The design was applied by painting or with a potato stamp in a manner resembling block printing. Red, blue, and yellow in soft native colors were used in these designs.

A potato stamp was made by cutting a potato in half and upon the flat surface picking out a design in relief by cutting away the background. The stamp was then dipped in dye and applied to the wider splints in the basket.

Collections of Iroquois handicrafts sometimes include miniature baskets the size of a thimble, made of the root of the gold thread plant (Coptis trifolia (L.) Salisb). Toy baskets were also carved from peach and plum stones. The Iroquois made many of these tiny objects. In addition to the small baskets, small bowls, miniature masks, and dolls were used as charms or by children in their play.

As late as 1875 baskets were being made in considerable quantities on the St. Regis reservation and were being sold among the neighboring White people. Today, however, basket making is carried on chiefly for use in the Iroquois homes.

The Dug-out Canoe. To secure a log out of which to make the wooden canoe or dugout, a circle of clay was applied near the base of a tree and a fire was started just below it. When the tree had been burned for a few inches the charred portion was scraped away with a stone chisel. It might be necessary to repeat the process several times until the tree was felled. The log was reduced to the desired length by charring and scraping and a cavity was hollowed out by further charring and scraping.

Mortar and Pestle. To make a wooden mortar for pounding corn the trunk of an oak or other hard wood tree was cut in the desired length and placed in an upright position. The top was hollowed out by first applying fire then cleaning the charred portion away by use of a stone chisel. The mortar was usually about two feet high and 20 inches in diameter, and had a symmetrical cavity at one end about 12 inches deep. A double-ended pestle or muller of hard maple, about four feet in length, was made to be grasped with both hands mid-

54. Iroquois corn mortar and pestle.

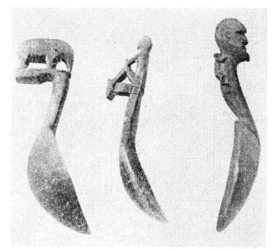

55. Carved wooden spoons: Seneca, Mohawk, Iroquois.

way of the handle, when in use. Two or three pestles were sometimes used in one mortar when pounding. A smaller mortar and pestle of wood were used to crush the sunflower seeds which furnished oil for food, for use on the hair and for anointing the false faces used in the ceremonies. The wooden mortar and pestle for grinding corn continue in use today.

Spoons and Ladles. Spoons and stirring ladles to be used for every day and for ceremonial purposes were carved out of the wood of the cherry, hard maple, white ash, apple, and horse chestnut tree. The handles were usually shaped to fit over the edge of the bowl or kettle so that the spoon would not slip in. Ducks, pigeons, and sleeping swans were favorite decorations at the ends of the handles. The bear and the dog were also popular on the carved objects. After being carved the spoons were boiled

in an infusion of hemlock bark or roots to produce a dark color.

The carving on the ladles or paddles made for stirring ceremonial meals shows especial skill; clan animals were often used as the design. An open-work pattern with a ball inside was carved on some of the handles. Such ladles were used in stirring the strawberries at the Strawberry Festival and the corn soup at the Green Corn Festival.

56. Seneca wooden spoons.

Snowshoes. Snowshoes were necessary for both hunting and warfare and were worn by the Iroquois for almost one-third of the year. They were built on a light frame of hickory with two or more bracing cross-

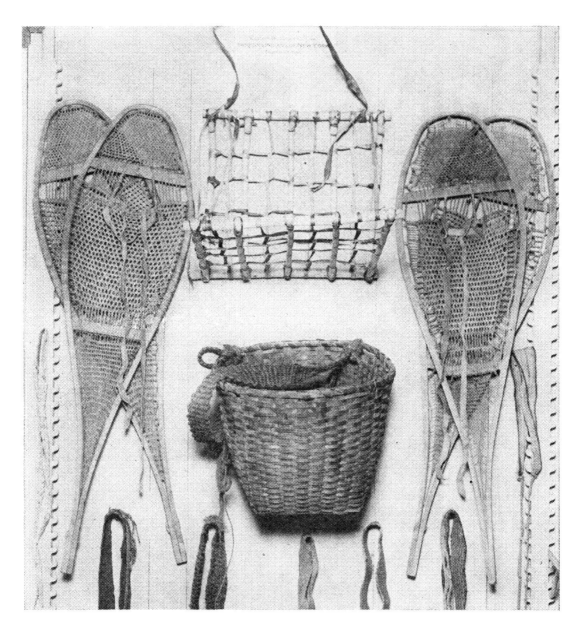

57. Snowshoes and burden baskets.

pieces (toe bar and the heel bar) to determine the spread and were filled in with a web or netting of sinew or skin thongs. They were usually nearly three times as long as wide, about three and one-half feet long and sixteen inches wide with a rounded or square toe. A pointed toe was sometimes used. A characteristic of the Iroquois snowshoe was that the space within the toe was usually left open without netting for walk-ing in soft snow.

After the men had prepared the frame of the snowshoe it was filled with a hexagonal web of moose or deer skin rawhide thongs. Three sets of parallel strands were made to cross each other at an angle of 120 degrees, with the result that the meshes are hexagonal in shape. One set of parallel strands was strung diagonally across the middle of the frame, the wrappings going

62

around the frame and bars. A set of parallel strands running diagonally in the opposite direction was strung in the same way. The third set of strands was then laced in with a needle crossing the intersections of the two previous sets. The needle was a piece of hard wood two and one half inches long with pointed ends and a hole in the center.

Thongs of the rawhide (babiche, French) were attached to the center crosspiece of the frame and were passed around the heel of the wearer to fasten the snowshoe to the foot. The heel was left free to move up and down and a small opening below the crosspiece allowed the toe of the foot to descend below the surface of the shoe as the heel was raised in the act of walking. The women wore a shorter, rounder snowshoe, with the netting extending throughout the frame.

An emergency snowshoe was constructed by bending a long twig the required shape and filling it with a netting of vegetable fibers.

59. Husk basket.

USE OF CORN HUSKS AND CORN COBS

At harvest time when the corn was gathered the Iroquois women sat in groups in the fields preparing the ears for storage. They turned the husks back and braided them firmly, forming a long rope from

58. Seneca corn husk foot mat.

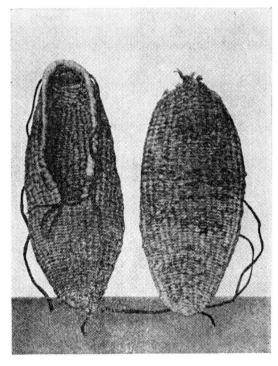

60. Seneca husk moccasins.

which the ears of corn depended. The braids formed an effective decoration as they hung either inside or outside the house while the corn was drying.

Corn husks were used for many purposes. They served as lamp lighters, as kindling to start a fire, as filling in pillows, cushions, mattresses, as water sprinklers, as cases in which to cook corn pudding, for clothes lines, and in the fashioning of many handicraft articles. By a technique of braiding, coiling, and sewing, the shredded husks were used to make mats, baskets, moccasins, masks, quivers for arrows, and dolls for ceremonial purposes.

Baskets and pouches of corn husks were tightly woven in various shapes. Watertight salt dishes and salt bottles were woven of corn husks. Later, bottles and jars were provided with net-like corn husk covers similar to woven covers on imported bottles.

Tightly woven corn husk moccasins were made to be used as over-shoes. They were oiled and stuffed with buffalo hair to provide warmth. Braided corn husk ankle bands were worn at the dances.

Corn cobs were used as stoppers for husk salt bottles and for closing the opening in corn husk rattles. Corn cobs served as scrubbing brushes and scratchers. As a fuel, corn cobs served to smoke meats and hides.

Corn Husk Mats. The corn husk sleeping or lounging mat is thought to have been used by the Indians prior to the coming of the Europeans. There are many references to the use of mats in the folklore of the agricultural tribes. The corn husk lounging mat was made up of rows of husks of equal length neatly rolled with the ends folded. The husks for the second row were inserted in the ends of the husks of the first row and tied or stitched in place with basswood cord. Thus row after row of husks was added. The finished mat showed a stitching of basswood cord crossing the corn husks at regular intervals several inches apart. The edge of the mat was finished with a tight husk braid.

Another type of mat was made from husks that had been loosely braided, coiled

61. Corn husk bed mat.

and sewed together with bark thread.

A thick husk door mat was made by braiding strands of the husks in such a way that on one side of the braid the ends were left protruding for an inch or more. The braid was then coiled to form a round or oval mat with the rough side on top. The coils were sewed together with corn husk or other fiber. When the mat was finished the protruding ends of the husks were neatly trimmed to form a short, stiff pile.

Corn Husk Dolls. Corn husk dolls with hair of corn silk were made both with and without facial features, to be used in certain medicine rites. Some of the dolls were without clothing. Others were dressed in skin or in the textiles used by the Iroquois after White contacts.

Arthur Parker gives the following description of the making of a corn husk doll. "Dolls are made by folding the husk in a pestlelike form for the neck and body. Room is left for the head and neck and the central core is pierced to allow a wisp of husk to be pulled through to be braided into arms. The lower portion is pierced in the same way and the husk for the legs pulled through. Husks are rolled around the upper portion of the neck and the head is formed. Husks now are placed over the back of the neck and carried diagonally across the chest from either side. The same process is repeated from the front and the husks drawn diagonally across the back. This produces the body and shoulders. The legs are then braided or neatly rolled into shape, wound spirally with twine, and tied tightly at the ankles. The foot is then bent forward at right angles to the leg and wound into shape. The arms undergo a similar process, but no attempt is made to simulate hands. The head and body are now ready for covering. For the head the wide husks are held upward against the top of the head and a string passed around them. The husks are then bent downward and the string tightened. This leaves a little circular opening at the top of the head. The head cover husks are drawn

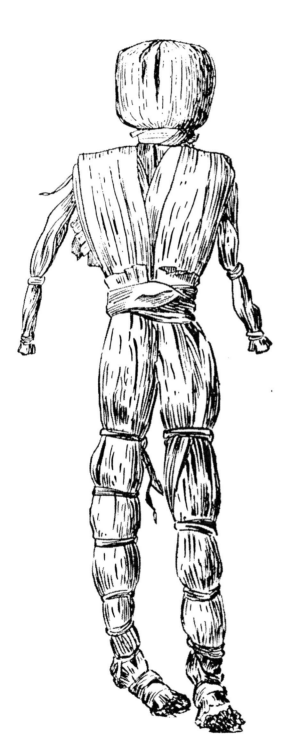

62. Corn husk doll.

65

tightly over the form and tied at the neck, which is afterward wound neatly with a smooth husk. More diagonal pieces are placed over the shoulders fore and aft and drawn tightly down to the waist. A wide band is then drawn around the waist and tied. The doll is now ready for corn silk hair which will be sewn on and its face may be painted. The dolls are sometimes dressed in husk clothing, but more often cloth or skin is used. Dolls are dressed as warriors or women and are given all the accessories, bows, tomahawks, baby boards or paddles, as the sex may require."

The corn husk doll was from six to ten inches in height as determined by the length of the corn husk. A small corn husk doll, four inches in length, made in obedience to a dream, was cast aside to carry away some malady.

Apple Face Dolls. A dried apple face was used on a corn husk doll to represent "Loose Feet," a spirit that grants wishes to little children. To make an apple face doll, an apple that was slightly green was peeled and cored. On one side it was gently moulded with the hand to produce features and then it was hung up to dry slowly, usually behind the stove. Each day as the apple dried the features were further moulded until they finally bore resemblance to a human face in miniature.

A small block of wood was carved for the neck and shoulders above which was left a piece big enough to fit in where the core had been removed. This supported the head and provided the means for connecting it with the body of the doll.

USE OF SILVER

The use of silver by the Iroquois dates from the seventeenth century when the French and Dutch came into the country with metallic instruments. Silver medals, gorgets, beads, earrings, finger rings, and other ornaments for personal adornment were popular among the western Iroquois during the colonial period and were lavishly used throughout the latter part of the eigh-

teenth century (1720-1850). They superseded the earlier ornaments of bone, copper, shell, and polished stones. Copper and wire bracelets, arm bands, brooches, and ear rings, bronze rings, and copper beads were worn up to the middle of the eighteenth century.

The Iroquois of New York were the leading makers of silver jewelry, with a silversmith in almost every Iroquois village. They followed a profitable trade which did not die out until about 1865. Silver arm and head bands for both men and women were also made by White silversmiths and sold in great numbers to the Indians. Silver medals and coins from land purchases were used in making the ornaments for personal wear. The coins and medals were pounded out on an anvil then cut into patterns with metal punches and chisels and decorated with incised, embossed, and open work designs. The incised or engraved designs included dots, straight lines, curved lines, fine zigzags, tiny triangles, sun, moon, and star symbols, hearts, and diamonds. Life forms were rarely used. Monograms and heads in full face or profile were often used on silver rings and medals.

Crosses. Crosses became popular after the coming of the Jesuits in 1654, but seem to have been used chiefly for ornamental purposes rather than their religious significance. Many of the crosses were plain, others had ornamental ends, some of which were decorated with floral designs. Among the larger pieces has been found a double barred cross. It resembles the archepiscopal, pectoral, or processional cross used in the church at that time.

Brooches. Brooches were the most numerous of silver ornaments and were used in abundance to fasten and to decorate the costumes of both men and women, as many as two or three hundred brooches being worn on one costume. The brooches were also used to decorate ribbons, head bands, and sashes and to fasten the wide band of broadcloth used on the baby's cradle board.

Design 1.

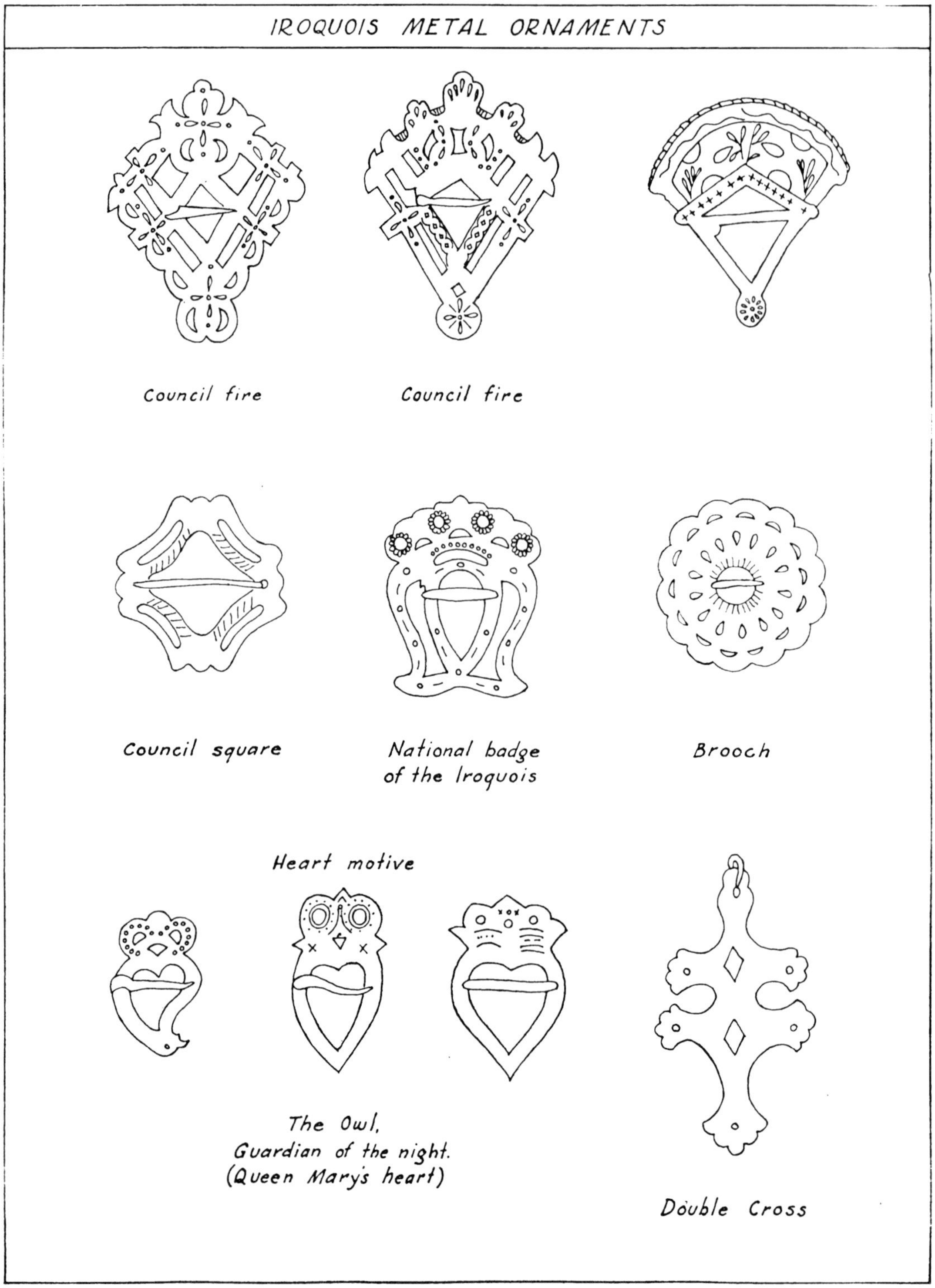
IROQUOIS METAL ORNAMENTS
Council fire
Council fire
Council square
National badge of the Iroquois
Brooch
Heart motive
The Owl, Guardian of the night. (Queen Mary's heart)
Double Cross

Design 2.

The number of brooches worn was indicative of the wealth of the wearer.

The brooch proper was a thin silver disk with a central opening across the front of which a silver tongue, loosely attached at one end, extended as on a buckle. The cloth could be pinched up in this central opening and the silver tongue passed through it to hold it in place.

Brooches varied in form, circumference, and size of aperture. Sometimes three inches in diameter, they were cut in various artistic forms on which designs were engraved, stamped, or embossed. The form and decoration of the brooches closely resembled the silver work of European origin.

TANNING HIDES

Deer Skins. The Indians had discovered that by tanning, a deer hide could be converted into a soft skin that was comfortable for robes and moccasins and offered a good foundation for the embroidered quill work in which the women excelled.

A rude knife of chert was used in skinning the deer. When the skin was to be tanned it was hung over a cylindrical beam while still fresh and the hair and grain of the skin were taken off with a wooden blade or stone scraper. In the later scrapers a piece of metal was inserted in the wood.

After scraping, the softened brains of the deer were spread on the skin. If it was necessary to keep the brains for some time before use, they were beaten up into a solution with moss which gave the mixture enough body to be made into cakes which were dried by the fire and kept until needed, sometimes for years. The brains of other animals and the spinal cord of an eel possess nearly the same properties as the deer's brains and were sometimes substituted for them. A mixture of eggs, corn meal, and water or young corn beaten to a pulp was occasionally substituted for the brain mixture in tanning. If a cake of the dried brain mixture was used, it was softened in boiling water and the moss, of no further use, was removed. The skin was soaked in the solution for several hours, after which it was wrung out and stretched many times until it became soft and pliable. If the skin were very thick it might be necessary to soak it several times so that it would become thoroughly penetrated by the solution. A fire was then built to form a smoke over which the skin was placed in such a manner that the smoke was all retained. Each side of the skin was smoked until the pores were closed and the skin had become thoroughly toughened and a light brown in

Iroquois runtees
(shell)

Design 3.

color. The finished skins were used for clothing, other personal articles, and for blankets or robes, which were popular with the White settlers as well as the Indians.

Bear Skins. Bear skins were dressed with the fur left on. They were first softened in a little clear water, then spread on a log so that the inner surface could be scraped to remove all the particles of flesh. The surface thus cleaned was then thoroughly rubbed with brains or a mixture of eggs, corn meal and water, great care being taken not to wet the fur side. When the skin was nearly dry it was worked until soft, back and forth over the smooth rounded top of a stake which had been driven into the ground.

The bear skin was used as an article of dress, as a robe or mattress to sleep on, or as a curtain at the door of the long house.

7

DECORATIVE ARTS

63. Seneca head dress.

The decorative arts of the Iroquois are much like those of the other Woodland Indians. Because of their early contacts with the White settlers the native work became demoralized and gave way to the fashioning of salable articles of commercial materials after patterns used by the Europeans. Skins were early replaced by broadcloth, calico, and silk. Moose hair and vegetable fibers gave place to commercial yarns in embroidery work. Porcupine quills gradually ceased to be used in decorative patterns as imported glass beads became available. Beads, originally used on skins, were applied to broadcloth, a combination that was popular for many years. Silk was used in applique and as a background for bead designs as early as the latter part of the eighteenth century (1762).

Moose Hair Embroidery. Hair from the mane, cheeks, and rump of the moose was used to embroider designs on both tanned skin and birch bark. The hair of the moose averages five inches in length. It is fine, dark brown in color at the outer tip, lighter at the center where it is a greenish tan, and white at the root end. The hair is lighter on the winter-killed moose. Moose hair takes dyes well and was often colored with the soft natural dyes when used in embroidery work.

Work done on buckskin or birch bark with the hair of the moose is to be found in many old collections. Delicate floral designs were usually developed with the moose hair. Occasionally the figure of a bird, animal or person was worked in.

Because of the fineness of the moose hair several hairs were used together in making embroidery stitches. Very fine over-and-over stitches were used to fasten them to the tanned hide or bark. Another technique shows the hairs inserted from the outside

64. Garter woven of bark or nettle cord, decorated with fine embroidery in moose hair.

of the skin or bark and carried through the material to the other side then with a short stitch back again and trimmed off evenly a short distance from the outer surface, much as a hooked rug is made.

Floral designs embroidered in moose hair on red broadcloth show strong French influence. Indian girls and women probably became acquainted with the French floral designs early in the seventeenth century when they studied under the nuns in the newly established French convents.

Quill Work. Quill weaving and embroidery were at one time among the arts practiced by the Iroquois. Their early skin robes, moccasins, and quivers were elaborately decorated with porcupine quills in woven or embroidered patterns similar to the work of the Northern Algonquian tribes (Ojibwa, Cree, and Ottawa). Quill work in birch bark was not developed to so great an extent by the Iroquois as among the other Woodland tribes and is not carried on today. Only a few examples of the woven quill work remain.

Fine geometric designs in well blended colors were developed in the weaving. Elaborate techniques that are no longer used were practiced.

In the embroidery work some delicate floral patterns were worked out with very fine, young quills, but most of the embroidery designs were geometric because of the stiffness of the quills.

The craft workers sorted the quills as to diameter and length, dyed them various colors as desired, and kept them in cases made from bladders of the elk or some other large animal. The undyed white quills, with their brown tips, were used effectively in working out the early designs.

In the quill embroidery, sinew was used as thread and a sharp thorn served as a primitive needle. A steel awl later replaced the thorn. When the quills were to be applied they were soaked for an hour or more in water, flattened between the teeth, then fastened to the skin with the sinew thread. Holes through which the sinew thread could be drawn were made in the buckskin with a fine awl. Patterns seem not to have been necessary to the early workers, but old tribal designs were used repeatedly.

Bead Work. The use of beads for personal adornment goes far back into prehistoric times. Beads of stone, bone, pottery, and shell have been found in old graves and in the excavations of village sites. Shell beads were made from the spiral center of sea shells (Columellea), pierced at both ends, apparently serving for necklaces and as costume decoration.

As in dealing with other native peoples, Columbus and his successors offered commercial beads to the Indians in exchange for riches of the new world. Records show that imported beads were supplied to the Mohawks as early as 1616, and beads are found in the excavations of the villages of that period. By the eighteenth century commercial beads were in common use. They had replaced both the quills and the small shell disks that had been previously used

72

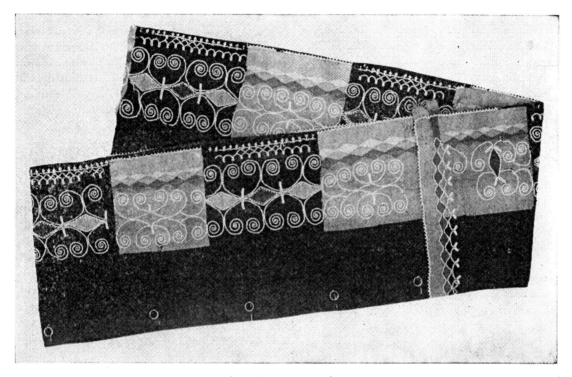

65. Cayuga woman's skirt.

for ornamental purposes. Commercial thread gradually replaced sinew.

Bead embroidery decorated both the skin and cloth articles of the Iroquois. The old quilled patterns were used in bead embroidery and the beads were attached to the skins with sinew, being couched down by use of the spot stitch as the quills had been. When the spot stitch was used two threads were necessary. The beads were strung on one thread, which was carried along in the direction desired, and was fastened down by a second thread which was carried across it after each two or three beads as desired. The threads were firmly drawn to hold the beads in place.

The use of thread and needle in the later bead work on cloth, made possible the working out of complicated curved designs so that the elaborate Iroquois bead patterns of later years bear no apparent relation to the simpler ones done on skins with sinew and awl in the earlier days.

Substitution of a new type of decoration apparently took place gradually, for on a few of the old pieces of handwork the three types of ornamentation are to be found—

quillwork, beadwork, and shell decoration.

During the last third of the nineteenth century in almost every St. Regis home some beadwork was being carried on, in many cases as a leisure time occupation, in a few as a regular industry with hired labor. Fancy articles in great variety were being made of bright colored cloth, embroidered with clear, glass beads. So completely had the work been commercialized that a sewing machine was often used to stitch up the seams in the cloth.

Ribbon Work. During the latter part of the eighteenth century ribbons began to appear in the costumes of the Iroquois. Though they did not develop the elaborate ribbon work patterns that were used by the Woodland tribes on the Great Lakes, the Iroquois made much use of ribbons applied as borders with a blind stitch or as a background for the white beads that decorated some of their later costumes. Effective color combinations were secured by the use of colored ribbon borders usually finished on both sides with one or more rows of white beads, and by using colored ribbons under beaded scrolls and flowers.

The ribbon work was used on skin moccasins and on broadcloth costumes, arm, wrist, and neck bands, and on bags and other costume accessories of both men and women.

Table Cloths, Bed Spreads, Blankets. The Indians were quick to apply their hand work to table covers, hand bags, pin cushions and other articles brought from Europe, using designs previously developed on such native articles as moccasins and bands for baby cradles. About 1860 they began to embroider floral designs in colored beads arranged to give shaded effects, an apparent copying of foreign decorative art forms. This heavy bead embroidery was much used by the Tuscarora on round ceremonial caps, bags of various shapes, and velvet moccasin cuffs.

Bed spreads, blankets, and table covers usually of red broadcloth were decorated with large floral designs in the center and deep curved borders of beads around the outer edge. These resemble the blankets which earlier were decorated with moose hair embroidery, but a much heavier design in the raised bead-work was used in the later Tuscarora work. The scalloped borders one and one-half inches or more in width, similar to those used on the side bags worn on a lady's belt, were made up of as many as ten rows of line beading in several colors, carried carefully around the curves. The outside edge was sometimes finished with a scalloped loop of white beads and the inside with white beads grouped in small effectively spaced pyramids. Fine beads were customarily used for these borders.

DESIGNS

The Iroquois used a wide variety of designs which show interesting contrasts, having been developed in different media, at different periods, under widely differing influences. Intertribal contacts, the coming of the colonists, and the introduction of new materials and new tools resulted in radical changes in design styles.

The early use of design can be studied on pieces of pottery and on wood-carving collected from old village sites. During the sixteenth and seventeenth centuries the Indians of New York State used geometric designs on their pottery. Groups of parallel straight lines in angular combinations were incised or carved in the clay. For a brief period, beginning in the latter part of the sixteenth century, animal forms were used. The bowls on the clay pipes of the Iroquois were modeled with a high degree of realism, human and animal forms being most commonly used. The modeled type of sculpture, rather than the carved type, found its greatest development among Indians in these Iroquois pipes.

To some extent the designs on wood resemble those on pottery. Wooden utensils were decorated with zigzag and other straight line designs. Geometric designs were followed by the more elaborately carved realistic figures that characterize many of the later Iroquois utensils.

Some of the oldest Iroquois designs are those found on "tump lines" or burden straps woven of vegetable fibers. They were geometric and included diagonal lines, rectangles, triangles and rhomboid designs all of which were usually "stepped" when worked out in the weaving. Similar designs are found in the wampum and woven yarn belts. Zigzag and V- or W-shaped patterns occur on the belts. The otter-tail pattern, so popular with the Indians of the Great Lakes, was often used by the Iroquois on the woven yarn sashes where it was worked out in white beads.

Quill and Bead Designs. The early quill designs were largely geometric, due to the stiffness of the quills and the technique used. On the woven or plaited quill work, used as bands and borders, zigzag and triangular patterns predominated. Long scroll designs were sometimes worked out in quills on the women's costume. The circle was often used as a unit design, filled in solidly with quills. Very fine floral de-

66. Woman's beaded leggings.

signs were used in some of the early quill embroidery work. Similar fine designs were embroidered with moosehair at an early date.

Geometric designs were less prominent in the later quill embroidery work. The double curve motif which was found in early quill embroidery work on leggings, moccasin flaps, skirts, and bags was gradually super-seded by floral designs.

The mythological turtle (on which the earth was built, having been brought up from a piece of mud), the crane, hawk, heron, bear, wolf, deer, snipe, and beaver were clan figures used as unit designs by the Iroquois. The animal that served as his clan symbol was pictured in embroidered quill or bead work on the skin robe, breech cloth or other part of the man's costume.

Distinctive Iroquois styles in bead embroidery patterns, usually common to all five nations, were developed with the new materials made available by the traders. White bead embroidery patterns with scroll motives used on the broadcloth and calico costumes are as characteristic of the Iroquois handicrafts as were the geometric designs worked out with such precision on the carefully woven tump lines of earlier generations. The styles and designs of the Seneca and the Cayuga are best known and are probably the most distinctive of the Iroquois handicraft productions.

Beaded Border Patterns. Striking designs developed as border patterns done in white beads on dark broadcloths are found on the leggings, robes, and women's costumes of the period 1750 to 1850. The finest of white seed beads were generally used in these border patterns, though larger beads of other types sometimes appeared, probably due to a change in the supply made available by the trader. Color, if used, was introduced by running silk ribbon along the edge of the garment under the beads, or by using a piece of colored silk as a background to the small diamonds or circles that were often present in the patterns. A floral or "flowering design" known as the "celestial tree, with all manner of fruit and flowers" often enriched one corner of the blanket or skirt and was usually partially done in delicately colored beads that harmonized with the colored ribbon used on the border. Light blue and old rose ribbon and beads were commonly used in this way in the borders.

75

A popular unit design consisted of an inverted semicircle resting upon two parallel, horizontal lines, having at the top two divergent curved lines each springing from the same point and curving outward like the end of a split dandelion stalk. The semicircle represented the sky dome, the parallel lines represented the earth, and the curved lines represented the celestial tree. In some patterns the curves occurred as a trefoil, in others as a double tree. Sometimes a sun with radiating rays occurred above the semicircle, with or without the celestial tree. The tree was still further elaborated by superimposing various other forms upon it.

The beaded border designs ranged all the way from rows of beads in straight lines or in simple, undulating curves to elaborately worked-out, lace-like patterns in which semicircles and scrolls predominated. The "pot-hook" or "scorpion" design was prominent in most of the patterns in which curves were used. The units of these elaborate designs were frequently based on a double curve motif similar to the Algonquin double curve. A balanced pattern was often repeated along the border. The double curve motif was used quite generally in the isolated designs such as are found on hair ornaments, bands for baby cradles, moccasin yokes, and knife sheaths.

The line designs used along the edge of the garments were done in a parallel arrangement, row after row, sometimes a half inch or more deep, occasionally in varied colors; or short lines were used in groups of three or five, radiating from circles, semicircles, or from curved borders; in other cases short lines were attached at intervals to the stems, in floral designs, giving the appearance of thorns. They may

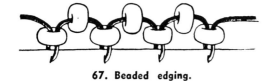

67. Beaded edging.

68. Embossed beading on man's cap.

have represented leaves or the sun's rays.

Sometimes a beaded row of small isosceles triangles was used in combination with the parallel lines that made up the border. If embroidered with very fine beads the triangular designs have a delicate, lacy effect. A deep lattice work, with the alternate diamonds partially crossed or stippled, frequently enriched the border design. The lattice design usually occurs in combination with the scroll or other curved designs.

Often semicircles were used in the border pattern to give a well defined scalloped design. More often the semicircles were combined with the lattice and radiating designs and were embellished with a simple hook design, frequently doubled, or with scrolls used singly or in groups of two or three. Concentric circles were used to represent both flowers and buds. Beads in two or more colors were often used in the concentric circles in alternating rows with a row of white beads between.

Beaded Edging. The white bead embroidered border patterns were almost invariably finished with a beaded edging which superseded the leather fringe used on the earlier garments. Sometimes on the less elaborate costumes the beaded edging was used alone without a border pattern. In forming the edge the beads were so arranged that every other bead stood out at right angles to the beads along the edge of the material, thus giving an effective finish to the garment. The edge of the garment was sometimes scalloped before being beaded, thus provid-

76

ing an especially handsome border. A great many beads were sometimes used in working out this border pattern to give a deeper edge.

Several different methods were employed to make the beaded edging. In the method most generally used the thread was passed through a bead then through the edge of the material and up through the first bead again. Two beads were then taken up on the thread before it was again passed through the material and up again through the last of the two beads. Two beads were again taken up on the thread and the work continued as before. In the finished edging the beads were alternately vertical and horizontal, the horizontal beads being those attached directly to the edge.

Embossed Beading. Heavy floral designs embroidered with the lazy stitch in beads of many colors are found on articles of velvet—on bags, caps, and moccasin vamps and cuffs. These embroidery designs differ from the border designs both in technique and in choice of colors. Though they probably arose from different sources they seem to have been used during the same period (1860-1890). The heavier designs were usually made with large beads. Opaque or pearl colored beads were popular. The beads were strung on sinew which was tacked to the skin by inserting it on the upper surface of the skin after a hole had been made by an awl. So large a number of beads was taken up on the sinew that they could not be drawn close to the skin when the sinew was again fastened to it, but were left raised in the finished embroidery. Sometimes padding was put underneath to hold them up, giving the finished pattern an embossed appearance.

SYMBOLISM IN DESIGNS

Because they lacked a written language the Iroquois used such memory aids as pictographs, wampum belts, wampum strings, and other symbols in the making of records and in affirming contracts and treaties. Tally cards were used for the less formal purposes. There was probably much symbolism in the designs which they used on their handicraft articles.

The feast bowl was decorated with beaver tail symbols which signified peace and plenty. Celestial, geographical, and mythical phenomena were represented by the design units known as the sky dome (the half circle), the sun (in conventionalized form), the horned trimmings (the scroll or helix), the celestial or evergrowing tree (in natural or geometric form), and the council fire (in the form of a hexagon or square).

In his Journal (1768-1782) John Long says "All these nations express peace by the metaphor of a tree whose top they say will reach the sun and whose branches extend far abroad not only that they may be seen at a great distance, but to afford them shelter and repose." The metaphorical pine tree of the Iroquois which served as the emblem

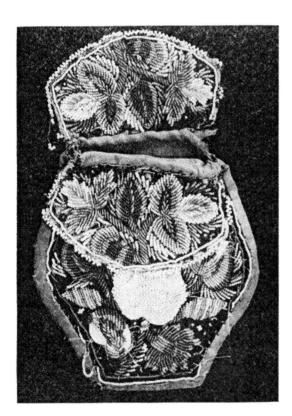

69. Beaded cloth bag.

of the confederacy was variously known as the Evergrowing Tree, the World Tree, the Great Earth Tree, the Tree of Life, the Tree of Peace and the Celestial Tree. It was thought to stand at the center of the world, bearing the sun and moon aloft in its branches. According to other legends it bore luminous blossoms that provided light for the "men beings" dwelling in the world. Its great white roots were believed to penetrate down to the primal turtle upon whose back the earth was thought to rest. The turtle was much used in old designs.

The scroll, helix, or tendril designs were called violets by the Tuscarora, literally, "bowing the head." The Tuscarora regarded them as a sign of good luck, deriving the idea from a children's game of locking the flower heads together. The Mohawks called the scroll designs "fern heads" and "horned" trimmings.

Another meaning read into the scrolls is that they denote horns of chieftancy, those curving outward denoting a living chief (life, living, light), those curved inward being emblematic of a dead chief (sleep, death). In more cases the curves in the Iroquois designs turned outward rather than inward. The antlers of a deer were the emblem of chieftainship. Anciently a chief wore horns in his headdress as the insignia of his rank or office and he "wears the horns" was a figurative expression for a chief. The chief who was deposed was spoken of as having been "de-horned."

The circle was among the oldest of the designs used in the quill embroidery. It was regarded as a symbol of life, its unbroken circumference being significant of the continuation of life in the world beyond. On some of the old buckskin robes the circle was embroidered in red quills, usually surrounded by a border in radiating lines done in quills of a lighter color. The red circles or disks were used on the front of the costume, usually one near each shoulder, or on the breech cloth.

Symbolism was expressed to some extent through the colors as well as by means of the designs. A sacred red paint was used in ceremonies. White beads were used to express peace, health, harmony. Dark purple or black beads represented sorrow, death, mourning, hostility. Red beads were used to make a declaration of war or to offer an invitiation to join in making war.

COLORS USED IN HANDICRAFT WORK

Old pieces of colored quill work indicate that the Iroquois knew much of natural dyes, but they began to make use of commercial dyes as soon as they were available and the soft colors of the native dyes were replaced by the harsher aniline dyes. Skins were sometimes dyed black. However, the Iroquois have chosen the more delicate shades in their quill embroidery work. Dyes from the walnut hull and the reddish brown skin of the onion continue to be used in Iroquois basketry.

Navy blue, turkey red, and green were popular colors in the calico, broadcloth, flannel, and ribbon selected for making the costumes. Most of the bead embroidered patterns were worked out in white beads against these strong backgrounds.

Colored beads were introduced into some of the circles and flowers, and colored silk was used for borders, usually with an edging of white beads. Old rose silk was much used with white beads.

When colors were used by the Iroquois they were usually harmoniously blended. Strong contrasts were avoided. White beads surrounded the colored beads and were used between colored beads of contrasting colors. Thus blue and pink were used with white between; dark blue and yellow with white between; light and dark purple with white between; and red and light blue with white between.

DYES AND THEIR PREPARATION

The art of dyeing was practiced chiefly by the women. Porcupine quills, elk hair, ash splints, vegetable fibers, and leather were among the materials dyed. Dyes were also used to darken wooden spoons and other wooden utensils. To prepare a dye for wooden spoons, hemlock bark or roots were boiled in water until the liquid was of the desired dark red shade, and then the spoon was plunged in and boiled until it had become thoroughly saturated with the dye and had acquired the desired color. With use and time the spoon became almost as dark as ebony and took on a high polish.

A few of the natural colors commonly used by the Iroquois and the materials that have been used for dyes, are listed below.

Brown was obtained from the husk or shuck of the butternut.

Black was made from the shuck of the butternut or the bark of the alder or maple in solution with sulphate of iron. From the shuck of the nut a brownish black was secured, from the bark of the alder a purplish black, and from the bark of the maple a bluish black.

Yellow was obtained from the seeds of the sweet gale (Myrica gale). The seeds were pounded, mixed in water, and boiled for about fifteen minutes. The material to be dyed was added and the boiling continued for another fifteen minutes. The material was then removed from the dye and washed, first in soap and water, then in pure water. It was then wrapped in flannel and dried. The yellow thus obtained was of pure hue, rather pale, but very durable.

Blue dye was extracted from green baize by boiling it in pure water. When the water was deep blue in color the material was introduced, together with a little powdered alum. Then the water was again brought to the boiling point, and the boiling was continued for fifteen minutes, after which the material was removed and washed in pure water. It was essential that the baize be old or much worn. It then retained its yellow and parted with its blue during the boiling.

Green was secured by first dyeing the material yellow, then boiling it in the blue decoction as when dyeing material blue.

Red dye was extracted from the root of the galium. The seeds of the sumac with their pericarp and the stalks to which they are attached, were washed in cold water to clean them. They were then boiled in soft water. When this water had attained a deep, brownish red, it was strained through flannel. The pulverized root of the galium was infused in the sumac water and the material to be dyed was introduced. The temperature was gradually raised to the boiling point, and kept there for several minutes. The material was then taken out and rinsed in soft water, after which it was soaked for a short time in weak soap and water. Then it was washed in pure warm water, wrapped up in flannel, and dried. This dye produced a deep, durable scarlet. If lighter tints were desired the time of infusion was shortened.

CONCLUSION

Even a cursory study of the Iroquois reveals them as an interesting people with a zest for life. They took a keen interest in tribal activities, in their religious observances, in sports, in their industrial and agricultural pursuits, and in their varied handicrafts.

Though their handicrafts show many distinctive features, the close relation of their work to that of other Woodland tribes is apparent in their use of bark containers, in their basketry, in their quill and bead work techniques, in their woven yarn sashes and in the ribbon work which ornamented their broadcloth costumes. However, the elaborate development of the scroll design in their white beaded borders gives to their costumes a characteristic finish that makes possible the recognition of Iroquois embroidery patterns wherever seen.

In spite of many years of White contacts tribal observances continue, testifying to the devotion of the Iroquois to their past and their love for the ways of their forefathers.

BIBLIOGRAPHY

Barbeau, Marius
Assomption Sash.
National Museum of Canada. Bulletin 93. Anthropological Series No. 24, Ottawa, Canada, 1939.

Beauchamp, William M.
Bulletins. New York State Museum, Albany, N. Y.
No. 16. Aboriginal Chipped Stone Implements of New York. 84 pp. 23 pl. 1897.
18. Polished Stone Articles Used by the New York Aborigines. 102 pp. 35 pl. 1897.
22. Earthenware of the New York Aborigines. 74 pp. 33 pl. 1898.
32. Aboriginal Occupation of New York. 172 pp. Map. 1900.
41. Wampum and Shell Articles Used by the New York Indians. 161 pp. 28 pl. 1901.
50. Horn and Bone Implements of the New York Indians. 107 pp. 43 pl. 1902.
55. Metallic Implements of the New York Indians. 92 pp. 38 pl. 1902.
73. Metallic Ornaments of the New York Indians. 120 pp. 37 pl. 1903.
78. History of the New York Iroquois. 337 pp. 17 pl. Map. 1905.
89. Aboriginal Use of Wood in New York. 185 pp. 35 pl. 1905.
Iroquois Games. Journal of American Folk Lore. Vol. IX, No. XXXV, Oct.-Dec. 1896. pp. 269-277.
Iroquois Women. Journal of American Folk Lore. Vol. XIII. April-June 1900. pp. 81-91

Catlin, George
See Donaldson, Thomas.

Clarke, John M.
Ethnology. Bulletin 158. New York State Museum. Specimens destroyed by fire. pp. 64-84, 8 plates. Albany, N. Y. 1911.
The Wampums of the Iroquois Confederacy. New York State Museum. Bulletin 121, pp. 85, 108-110 with 12 plates. Albany, N. Y. 1908.

Clarke, Noah T.
The Thatcher Wampum Belts of the New York State Museum. New York State Museum. Bulletin 279. pp. 53-58. Albany, N. Y. 1929.
The Wampum Belt Collection of the New York State Museum. New York State Museum. Bulletin 288, pp. 85-121. Albany, N. Y. 1934. Reprint available.

Converse, Harriet M.
The Iroquois Silver Brooches. New York State Museum. 54th Annual Report. Vol. I, pp. r231-r254. 10 plates. Albany, N. Y. 1900.
The Seneca New Year and Other Customs. Indian Notes. Museum of the American Indian. Heye Foundation. Vol. 7. pp. 69-83, New York City, N. Y. 1930.

Converse, Harriet M. and Parker, Arthur C.
Iroquois Myths and Legends.
New York State Museum. Bulletin 125. pp. 5-190. Albany, N. Y. 1908.

Culin Stewart.
Games of the North American Indians. 24th Annual Report. Bureau of American Ethnology. Smithsonian Institution, Washington, D. C. 1902-3.

Donaldson, Thomas
The George Catlin Indian Gallery in the United States National Museum. Smithsonian Report. 1885. pp. 154-199. Washington, D. C. 1887.

Douglas, Frederic H.
Leaflets. Department of Indian Art, Denver Art Museum, Denver, Colorado. 1930-1940.
No. 12. The Iroquois Long House
26. Iroquois Foods
31. Iroquoian and Algonkin Wampum
51-52. Indian Linguistic Stocks or Families
62. Design Areas in Indian Art
65-66. Types of Indian Masks
67. Basketry Construction Technics
81. Tribes of the Great Lakes Region
87. Indian Basketry East of the Rockies
101. Tribal Names: Part 3.
102. Birchbark and the Indian
103. Porcupine Quillwork
104. Main types of Indian Metal Jewelry

Fenton, William N.
Contacts between Iroquois Herbalism and Colonial Medicine. Smithsonian Institution Annual Report. 1941. pp. 503-526.
Masked Medicine Societies of the Iroquois. Smithsonian Institution Annual Report. 1940. pp. 397-429. 25 plates.
An Outline of Seneca Ceremonies at Cold Spring Longhouse. Publications in Anthropology. No. IX. pp. 3-33. Yale University Press. New Haven, Conn. 1936.
The Seneca Society of Faces.
The Scientific Monthly. Vol. XLIX. pp. 215-238. March 1937.
Tonawanda Longhouse Ceremonies.
Ninety Years after Lewis Henry Morgan. Anthropological Papers. No. 15, pp. 139-165, Bulletin 128. Bureau of American Ethnology. Smithsonian Institution, Washington, D. C. 1941

Fletcher, Alice C.
Indian Education and Civilization. 1888.
p 565. Beadwork and basketry of the St. Regis Indians.

Harrington, M. R.
Iroqouis Silverwork.
American Museum of Natural History, Anthropological Papers, Vol. I, Part VI, pp. 353-369. 6 plates. New York City, N. Y. 1908.
The Last of the Iroquois Potters.
New York State Museum. Bulletin No. 133. Fifth Report of the Director of the Science Division. pp. 222-227. University of the State of New York, Albany, N. Y. 1909.
Seneca Corn Foods and Their Preparation.
American Anthropologist, 1908, Vol. 10, No. 4, New Series, pp. 575-590.

Hewitt, J. N. B.
Iroquoian Cosmology.
Part I, 21st Annual Report, 1899-1900. (p. 151 description of tree). Part II. Forty-third Annual Report. Bureau of American Ethnology. Washington, D. C. 1928.

Wampum.
Handbook of the American Indian, Bulletin 30, Vol. 2, pp. 904-909. Bureau of American Ethnology, Smithsonian Institution, Washington, D. C. 1912.

Hill, Cephas and Fenton, William N.
Reviving Indian Arts Among the Senecas.
Indians at Work. Vol. II. No. 21, pp. 13-15. June 15, 1935, Indian Office, Washington, D. C.

Holmes, William H.
Aboriginal Pottery.
20th Annual Report, pp. 159-175. 4 plates. Smithsonian Institution, Washington, D. C. 1898-99.

Lismer, Marjorie
Seneca Splint Basketry.
Indian Handcraft Pamphlet No. 4. United States Indian Service. Washington, D. C., 1941

Morgan, Lewis H.
Fabrics, Inventions, Implements and Utensils of the Iroquois.
Appendix. Fifth Annual Report of the Regents of the University. The State Cabinet of Natural History, pp. 67-117. Albany, N. Y., 1852.
League of the Ho-de-no-sau-nee or Iroquois.
Sage and Brother, Publishers. Rochester, N. Y., 1851. New edition. Edited and annotated Herbert M. Lloyd. 2 vol. Dodd, Mead, and Company. New York City, N. Y. 1901.
Report to the Regents of the University upon the Articles furnished the Indian Collection.
December 31, 1849. Third Annual Report of the Regents of the University. Albany, N. Y. January 11, 1850

Museum Service.
The Indian Arts Project
Museum of Arts and Sciences, Rochester, N. Y. Vol. 9, No. 1. January 15, 1936. p 8, 9.

Orchard, William C.
Beads and Beadwork of the American Indians.
Indian Notes and Monographs. Contributions, Vol. 11, pp. 1-140. Part of an Iroquois Sash, p. 116. Museum of the American Indian, Heye Foundation, New York City, N. Y. 1929.
Indian Porcupine-Quill and Beadwork
Introduction to American Indian Art. Part II, pp. 3-13. The Exposition of Indian Tribal Arts, Inc. New York City, N. Y. 1931.
Mohawk Burden Straps.
Indian Notes. Vol. VI, No. 4, pp. 351-359. Museum of the American Indian, Heye Foundation, New York City, N. Y. 1929.
The Technique of Porcupine Quill Decoration Among the Indians of North America.
Contributions. Vol. IV. No. 1. Museum of the American Indian, Heye Foundation, New York City, N. Y. 1916. Out of print.

Parker, Arthur C.
The Amazing Iroquois.
Art and Archaeology Magazine. 1927. Vol. 23, No. 3, pp. 99-108. Photographs of Indians, belt, pot.
An Analytical History of the Seneca Indians.
Researches and transactions of the State Archaeological Assocation. Published by the Lewis H. Morgan Chapter. Rochester, N. Y. 1926.
The Archaeological History of New York in Two Parts.
Bulletin 235-236 and 237-238, 743 p., 234 pl. 88 fig. New York State Museum, Albany, N. Y. 1920.
Art Reproductions of the Seneca Indians, Museum Service.
Museum of Arts and Sciences, Rochester, N. Y. Vol. 14, No. 9. Nov. 1941, pp. 31-33.
Certain Iroquois Tree Myths and Symbols.
American Anthropologist. N. S. Vol. XIV, No. 4, 1912, pp. 608-620.
The Code of Handsome Lake, the Seneca Prophet.
Bulletin 163, 148 p., 23 pl. New York State Museum, Albany, N. Y. 1913.
Iroquois Uses of Maize and other Food Plants.
Bulletin 144. 119 p., 31 pl., 23 fig. New York State Museum, Albany, N. Y. 1910.
The Origin of Iroquois Silversmithing.
American Anthropologist. N. S. Vol. XII, No. 3, pp. 349-357. 1910.
Secret Medicine Societies of the Seneca.
American Athropologist, N. S. Vol. XI, No. 2, April 1909, pp. 161-185.
Seneca Myths and Folk Tales,
Buffalo Historical Society, Publications No. 27. N. Y. 1923. 465 p. Appendix D. Emblematic Trees in Iroquoian Mythology, p. 431-444.
Seneca Woodcarving.
Museum Service, Museum of Arts and Sciences, Rochester, N. Y. Vol. 13, No. 5, May 1940. pp. 75, 76.
Snow-snake as played by the Seneca-Iroquois.
American Anthropologist. N. S. Vol. XI, No. 2, April-June, 1909, pp. 250-256.

Perry, C. Carleton
Indian Arts and Crafts Project
Museum Service. Museum of Arts and Sciences, Rochester, N. Y. Vol. 11, No. 8. Oct. 15, 1938. pp. 172, 173.

Ramusio, Giovanni Battista
Delle Navigationi et Viaggi,
1606, Venetia edition. Vol. III, Engraving p 380 (2 & 3).

Skinner, Alanson B.
Notes Concerning New Collections.
Iroquois Material.
Iroquois Burden Strap
Anthropological Papers. American Museum of Natural History. Vol. IV, Part II, pp. 278-281, New York City, N. Y., 1910.
Some Seneca Masks and Their Uses.
Indian notes, Vol. II, No. 3, pp. 191-207. Museum of the American Indian. Heye Foundation, New York City, New York. 1925.

Speck, Frank G.
Notes on the Material Culture of the Huron.
American Anthropologist. N. S. Vol.. 13, 1911. (Technique of netting, snowshoes, p. 219)

Speck, Frank G. and Orchard, William C.
Penn Wampum Belts.
Indian Notes and Monographs. Leaflet 4, Museum of the American Indian, Heye Foundation, New York City, N. Y. 1924-5.

Waugh, F. W.
Iroquois Foods and Food Preparation.
Canada Geological Survey, Memoir 86, Anthropological Series, No. 12, Ottawa, Canada, 1916.

Willoughby, C. C.
A Mohawk (Caughnawaga) Halter for Leading Captives.
American Anthropologist, N. S. Vol. 40, January-March 1938. pp. 49-50. Plate I.

From woman's costume

Bag Design

From knife sheath

From moccasin yoke

From mans tunic

Design 4.

Quilled design from
a moccasin toe

A design used in quill
weaving

Quilled design from a moccasin flap

Quill border on an old bag

Floral design

Double curve design

Design 5.

Design 6.

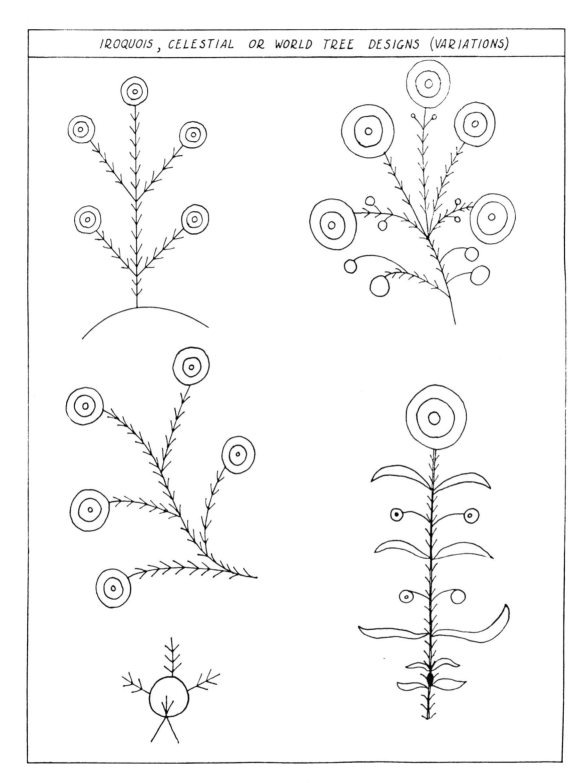

Design 7.

85

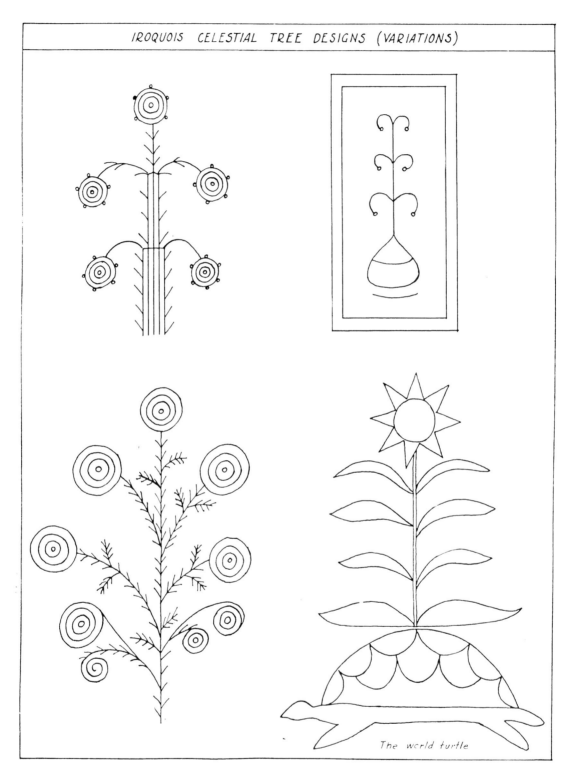

The world turtle

Design 8.

86

Iroquois belt embroidered in fine white beads

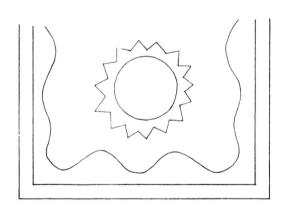

*Design from a Seneca breech cloth
embroidered in white beads*

Design 9.

87

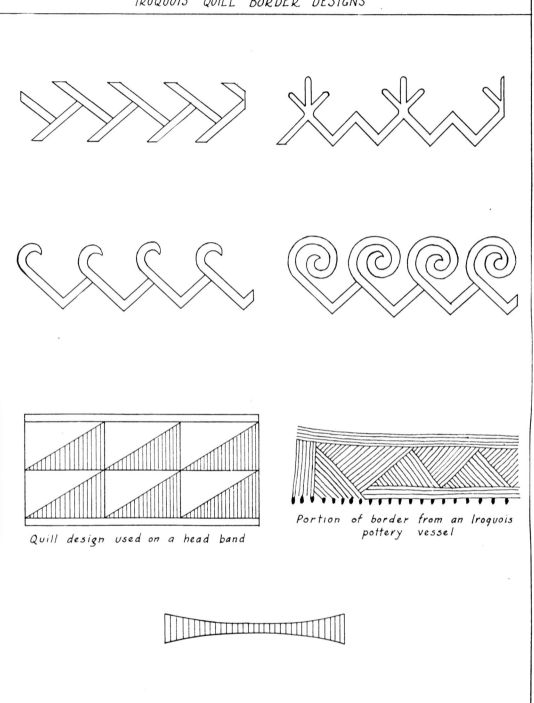

Quill design used on a head band

Portion of border from an Iroquois pottery vessel

Design 10.

Design 11.

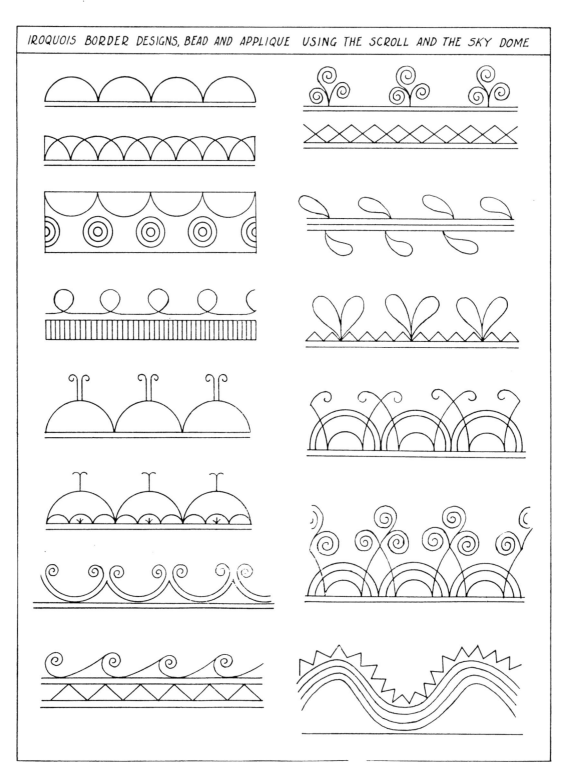

Design 12.

90

Design 13.

91

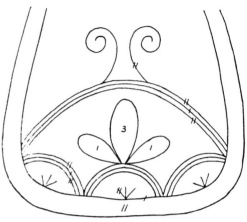

Embroidered yoke on Seneca woman's costume (white beads)

Seneca breech cloth design, worked out in beads and silk ribbon.

Design from Seneca woman's costume - embroidered in white beads.

Design 14.

IROQUOIS BORDER DESIGNS, BEAD AND APPLIQUE

Design 15.

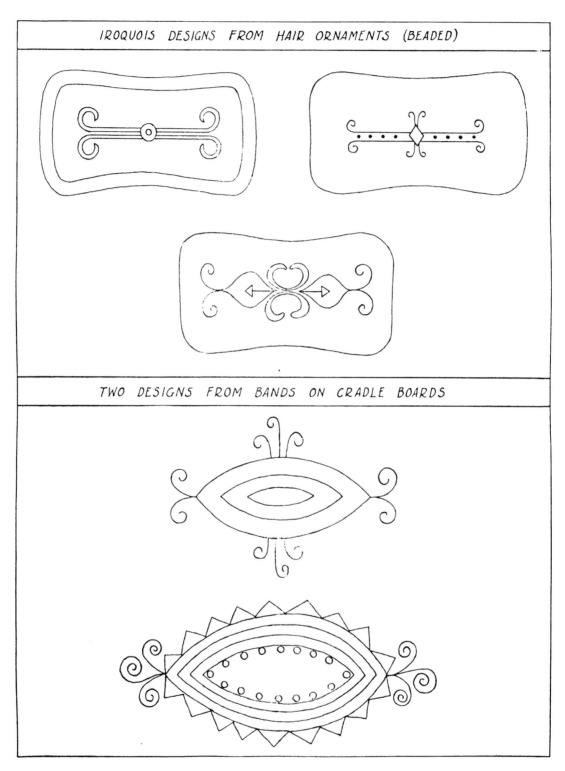

IROQUOIS DESIGNS FROM HAIR ORNAMENTS (BEADED)

TWO DESIGNS FROM BANDS ON CRADLE BOARDS

Design 16.

Design 17.

Design 18.

96

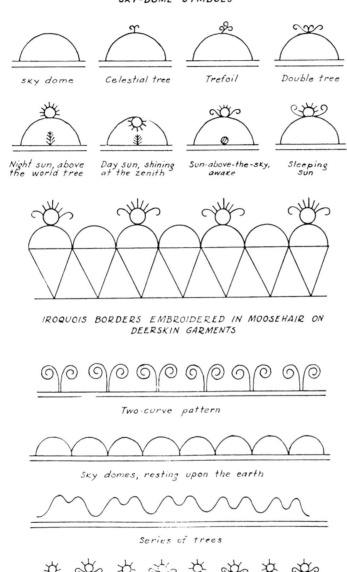

SKY-DOME SYMBOLS

sky dome   Celestial tree   Trefoil   Double tree

Night sun, above the world tree   Day sun, shining at the zenith   Sun-above-the-sky, awake   Sleeping sun

IROQUOIS BORDERS EMBROIDERED IN MOOSEHAIR ON DEERSKIN GARMENTS

Two-curve pattern

Sky domes, resting upon the earth

Series of trees

Suns and celestial trees resting upon the sky-dome

From – Arthur C. Parker, Certain Iroquois Tree Myths and Symbols

Design 19.

97

CPSIA information can be obtained at www.ICGtesting.com
Printed in the USA
BVOW052329170613

323594BV00003B/257/P